I0137547

Finding Your Sweet-Spot in the World of Healthcare

Creating a Life and Career You'll Love

C. J. SNOW

On the cover: The author living in her sweet-spot, photo taken in her Montana backyard under a double rainbow.

Copyright © 2024 C. J. Snow.

Copyrighted material, reproduction or dissemination
of any content only by written permission of author.

ISBN: 979-8-89079-214-3 (hardcover)
ISBN: 979-8-89079-215-0 (paperback)
ISBN: 979-8-89079-216-7 (ebook)

**Hardcover, paperback and eBook copies
can be purchased at cjsnow.net and Amazon.**

BULK DISCOUNTS OFFERED ON CJSNOW.NET

Table of Contents

Living In The Sweet-Spot

"My mission in life is not merely to survive, but to thrive; and to do so with some passion, some compassion, some humor and some style"

~ Dr. Maya Angelou

* * * ⭐ * * *

"We are what we repeatedly do; excellence, then, is not an act but a habit."

~Aristotle

* * * ⭐ * * *

"To change one's life:

1. *Start Immediately*
2. *Do it flamboyantly*
3. *No exceptions"*

~ William James

Dedication

It is with deep, heart-felt gratitude that I present this book as visible thanks to all the people who have contributed to my life and career, and to my husband who has been my best friend and supporter through our many years of marriage and the writing of this book. All of you have taught me things about maximizing life's opportunities, which has enabled me to create a life I love and feel deeply satisfied by. Your wisdom, encouragement and kindnesses I will always remember. You may have seen your part as small, almost insignificant acts of just "doing what you do," because you are simply in the habit of offering your best, because you have learned how to survive difficulties with grace, thrive wherever you are, always endeavoring to excel in life and assisting others to do the same. If I can inspire others a fraction of how you have inspired me, then I will have succeeded.

Be patient toward all that is unsolved in your heart
and try to love the questions themselves
like locked rooms and like books
that are written in a very foreign tongue.

Do not now seek the answers,
because you would not be able to live them
and the point is,
to live everything.

Live the questions now;
perhaps you will then gradually,
without noticing it,
live along some distant day into the answer.

Resolve to be always beginning
to be a beginner.

R. M. Rilke

BEGINNING

BEGINNING

... 1 ...

The Need To Put It All Down On Paper

"Write what should not be forgotten."

Isabel Allende

IT BEGAN AS a routine work day. At the time I had more than twenty years' experience as an RN in Emergency and Intensive Care Medicine. I was loving my career more than ever because I was *finally* working as a flight nurse aboard a helicopter for an outstanding company. I was very proud to be part of its team, and we were pressed on a daily basis to do our job with excellence...more than pressed, we *were passionate* about being the best we could be. Little did I know that over the course of the next forty-six hours I would be forever changed, impacted in a way I never imagined.

I had always been tough when it came to dealing with the tragedies that occur in this line of work, but the trifecta of events that presented over the course of that shift brought me to my knees. The full story of that experience I will share later in the book, but the essence of it is centered around three separate cases; all involving children, so uniquely different and heart-wrenching in their tragedy, that I found my usual capacity

3

to cope had abandoned me. Who would have thought that an experience such as this would have so much to teach me? It taught me how to be even more resilient, about the true character of what it takes to sustainably thrive at work and how to create my own sweet-spot both in the world of healthcare and in my personal life.

I never expected to be so dismantled by that day, yet that's where I landed. There have been many difficult and wonderful experiences that have shaped me over the course of my career, but it was this darkest moment that propelled me, as if by some primal instinct, to dig deep into how I "did life." It was simply a matter of survival to go there. I have always been an introspective person, but it was in the process of emerging from that difficult and unfamiliar place that I began to appreciate, at a deep and profound level, what sort of things contribute to my resilience and provide me with true, deep and lasting satisfaction. Like any good researcher, I began to really take stock of what worked and what didn't serve me. It was a powerful catalyst that recommitted me to live my life more consciously, making the most of every moment, thirsting for more understanding about what creates happiness.

Putting forth that effort allowed me to continue on the flight line for many years after and altered dramatically how I experience life as a caregiver. That personal endeavor to improve the way in which I approached life, helped me find harmony in a career that had often challenged my equilibrium. Finding that place gave me balance, granted me the thrill of achievement, and bestowed satisfaction and peace, both personally and professionally. My life became a place where I owned and actively created my existence, instead of living a life that was just happening and owning me.

Life is full of surprises. Who knew such a thing would have me begin such a journey and compel the need to write it all down? It took several years to get to the point where "what should not be forgotten" arrived on the pages before you, and it has been as much a gift to myself as it is an offering to you.

I never imagined that the process of writing would give me so much, but it gave me the altitude to see the gifts in difficulties. The journey clarified for me the solid principles of my own brand of excellence, unique to me and how, in the humble offering of it to the world, I feel content.

When I began writing this book, I had been working in the trenches as a frontline caregiver for more than twenty six years. I'd held many roles over my career, but direct patient care seems to be the place that satisfied me most. At that time I was employed by a large healthcare system in an urban emergency department that ranked in the top 4% of busiest ED's in the country. In spite of more than a few days where I grumbled a bit over the job's demands, I had arrived at a place where I really loved my work, my patients AND my life. I had managed to find a sweet spot, one where I was still excelling and felt immensely fulfilled in all my life roles, rooted in the commitment to, and cultivation of, my own personal best. It was a way of being where I was now habitually applying that principle to all parts of my life. It wasn't that I was successful in every endeavor, it was a sense of genuine authenticity that provided me peace and a deep happiness, even when facing the rigors of the job, life challenges, and my own imperfections and failures.

An average day in healthcare can be tough. Like many of today's jobs, whether medically related or not, the pressure can be immense. We pedal as fast as we can, endeavoring to get it all right, and sometimes it feels as though we will never catch up. Such a life can feel devoid of satisfaction because we so often feel like not enough or good enough has been achieved. I began appreciating as I structured the book's content that learning how to balance my life while offering my best had been key.

"Excellence" seems to be a current top-shelf word. It is used in many industries and often found in mission statements, designed to inspire public confidence with hope that we, the frontline folks delivering care or producing widgets, will also be inspired to offer our best. Mustering that kind of inspiration in staff can be difficult given the ever-increasing demands and other influences found in life. Customer expectations, rapidly changing technology and fast-paced advancements all challenge our fortitude. In most patient-care arenas, the job could never be recommended as easy money. Often the work has elements that are less than pleasant and sometimes goals can seem impossible to achieve.

When it came to this book it felt risky to include the word excellence; risky because I thought some of you might incorrectly think this is some sort of preachy, impractical, "better-than-you" compilation that demanded we be flawless. I wrestled with even discussing it, but in the end, how I have come to know excellence and the lasting satisfaction it brings was at the core of discovering my sweet-spot. As you may have guessed by now, my meaning of excellence has room for our humanity. Achieving excellence is largely an internal journey, because the validation for having achieved must come primarily from within. It's that knowingness of the ever-watching soul-self which acknowledges when we consistently present to the world the best version of ourselves.

My vision for the book was a down to earth approach, one that capitalized on my life experience with raw honesty; some bits shared with pride, others not so much. I think you'll find things we share in common and find the suggestions for improving life experience practical and within reach. Whether you are in medicine or not, I think you will find much of it familiar, relatable, and practical to apply.

Having recently crossed my thirty-five year mark as a registered nurse, I want to be frank and tell you that there were plenty of places that contained elements of discontent and some moments where I'd wished I'd done something differently. I did not always feel inspired; there were periods of burn out and bitter feelings that my career was not offering what I had hoped for. Over the years I have found myself asking many questions about how I could change my experience. Should I change jobs? Maybe it's just the people I'm working with? Or, maybe I'm just not as good as I should be at this and should change careers?

The management positions I have explored on occasion did not seem to satisfy me, nor did they seem to fit my best talents and abilities. What to do then? I came to find, several jobs and people later, that the difficulties were not so much in circumstances, but within me and within the perspectives I held. I don't mean just those perspectives I had at work, it was the whole shebang. No corner in my life was isolated from the others. All had varying degrees of influence on the whole.

I also want you to know that I still have occasional struggles and frustrations to maintain a positive perspective. I am not perfect. I have to work at making the positive my reality. It takes effort to accept that I am imperfect when I make a mistake or when I get off track from my ideals. But when it's all said and done, the bulk of my life feels authentic and committed to my core values, one where the intentional application of my best holds the possibility of making any moment exceptional, even in the context of my imperfect humanness.

All of us struggle to some degree. I hear my colleagues express their unhappiness. I feel their angst and know their desire for it all to be somehow easier. I have witnessed how we sometimes turn on each other as we blunder about trying to resolve such things. These are not unique to medicine, they are frequenters of our human experience and what has become a hardwired tendency to assign guilt or innocence. This further motivates me to share what changed me profoundly. Perhaps in sharing these discoveries I can help others to be more resilient, have a greater depth of happiness, create a greater sense of ease and workplaces where we feel happy and supported. It's not that I'm a declared expert on the concepts of mindfulness, integrity or conflict management that we will discuss, nor am I a degreed psychologist. What I do offer about these things comes from the perspective of someone who's been through the mill, who's studied the experts and worked at my own personal growth to gain insight for successful change. At the root of it all is a singular principle: *giving my best effort*. To consistently apply what I've learned is what has me surviving my missteps with more grace, thriving, and excelling more than ever before in my life. That effort fuels my own brand of excellence, and subsequently my resilience and overall happiness, even when missing the mark. In these pages you will hear the voice of someone who has graduated (many times,) from the school of hard knocks. Mistakes, hardships and humbling experiences have often been my greatest teachers. It has taken some courage to put my humanness down on paper, but with that bravery I believe I can make a difference.

So I began to write.

My initial focus was to write solely for my medical colleagues, especially the nurses who directly care for others, as they are nearest and dearest to my heart and where my personal experience lies. But while writing, and as reiterated by my editors, I realized that no matter what one's position in life, we are all somehow caretakers of others, or at very least caretakers of ourselves. Most of the things we'll explore universally apply, no matter what it is we do for a living or how we live our personal lives. Wherever you are on your journey, I hope you'll find in these pages things that resonate with you, things that will add to your own survival kit for navigating whatever demands you encounter. For those of you in medicine, I think you'll certainly find familiar territory and some new angles to consider.

We can all have a life and career that is cherished, that we are proud of and feel a deep sense of purpose in. The satisfaction of excellence—when living in our own unique and individual sweet-spot—is within our reach.

When Grabbing 100% Of My Career Wasn't Enough

Many of us pour our whole selves into our work. I have worked diligently to hone my nursing skills to a high level in critical care. I thought I had been to the top of my career mountain during my ten years in the intense world of flight medicine. Responding to scene calls and transporting the sickest of the sick from hospitals to specialty services was both challenging and thrilling—and

I absolutely loved (and still miss) flying in a helicopter. The work pushed me to another level of achievement I had not imagined myself capable of. Yet even with all that achievement and external validation, there still was a void, a lack in my life that had me feeling incomplete, at times burned out and occasionally struggling in a variety of ways. I was indeed grabbing for that 100% in my career. The trouble was my career was not 100% of my life.

This is how I began to understand how critically important it was to apply certain principles and effort to ALL of life. I discovered that being connected to others and staying connected to my own core values was equally, if not more important, than all my achievements as a nurse. All of my life needed the intention to excel if I wanted it to work. This all-inclusive approach created a wholeness and balance in my life that was necessary to create that profound satisfaction, that kind of contentment where true and consistent happiness was finally revealed. Though it may sound like a lot more effort to achieve that, it wasn't. Happiness in career and life, as it turned out, was far simpler than I ever thought and was more about living with greater awareness than it was about incorporating new things. It was this all-inclusive approach that made it manageable. It was separating the various parts of my life into silos that had made it complicated and dysfunctional.

How Did It Begin For You?

Most of us can tell a story about why we chose to pursue our line of work. It is in the heart of those stories that we can glimpse the idealized version of who we wanted to become. A common thread that many of our stories hold is the desire to achieve a meaningful existence; one where we exhibit something uniquely our own that is in some way special, where we excel and leave our mark on the world. Consider for a moment before reading on, what events or experiences influenced you to where you are now?

My own interest in medicine began at an early age, experiencing my grandfather as a physician in the small town of

Carpinteria, California. His compassion for people, commitment to being the best physician he could be, and his deep passion for medicine were mesmerizing. We'd hear his stories and watch his routines. Just being in his presence seemed to be healing. He'd go to the office or to the hospital to see patients until noon, then come home for lunch. After his meal he'd go to what he called his "kiva," which was a room at the end of the house where he had his library, his desk, his journals and a very comfy lounge chair. He would read a journal article or two while smoking his pipe, followed by a brief nap. We children were under strict instructions never to disturb him during this ritual. Precisely at 2:00 PM he would rise from the lounger and be off to see more patients. Late afternoons and evenings were reserved for house calls or the Friday night local football game as the team's physician.

Everyone called him "Doc," "Doc Coshow," or our family title: "Grandpa Doc." The simple truth was that he saw himself as a servant of humankind. When he saw a need, he found a way to fulfill it. Whether it be an ambulance for the community or a medical library for the hospital, he made it his business to make things happen. He didn't sit back and bemoan the lack, he set about working with the resources available to fill the need. He was always ready to roll up his sleeves and get to work, offer a smile of encouragement or some thoughtful words of advice. His levity was a tool he often used in an effort to lift people's spirits and lighten up about life. I remember how people's faces would light up when seeing him, he was like a relief valve in a serious world. It was through these various approaches that he was able to create positive change again and again. He embraced whatever he encountered in life, he loved and nurtured his family in a way that we all experienced deeply. He also was an adventurer, a gardener, historian and Sunday dinner prankster. (I will never forget his theatrical use of an amputation hand saw to carve Grandma's roast!) Grandpa Doc was indeed a master at grabbing 100% of his life.

Grandpa also taught me that we should be who we say we are, right down to the core, no matter what the cost. "Pioneers get arrows!" he used to say and he just expected an arrow or two to come his way when he forged new trails or spoke up on an unpopular subject. He would patiently massage an issue and people would respond. It was in this way that he became an integral part of his community. This was the man who first taught me about excellence and inspired me to practice the art of caring for people.

CARPINTERIA VALLEY MUSEUM OF HISTORY

Taken in the late 1930s, this photograph depicts Carpinteria's first ambulance, a vehicle purchased and adapted into an ambulance by the Lions Club. Pictured with the new rig are Ray Denno, school teacher; Dr. Horace Coshow, medical doctor; Sally Maddox, grocer/custodian/ ambulance driver; Wilbur Humphrey, Chevrolet dealer; Vic Stubbs, cement contractor; Emmanual Solari, rancher; Jack Wullbrandt, judge; and Jerome Tubbs, judge.

"Grandpa Doc," the third from the left, with his fund-raising Lion's Club members who worked to make the purchase of this ambulance possible. (Don't worry; the Lioness on the top was not a permanent fixture!)

Many of my career struggles came from my grandpa-fostered idealism and his "do the right thing" perspective—sometimes without regard for the personal cost at stake. What got me in trouble was that I did not inherit all the wisdom that accompanied my Grandfather. My impatience for change and lack of measured diplomacy has been a serious complication for me. I recall a scene in my junior high French class where some kids in the back of the class were bullying a girl. I abruptly stood up knocking over my chair in the process and yelled loudly at the kids to knock it off. My French teacher promptly grabbed me by the ear and hauled me off to the principal's office! Brave? Yes. Wise approach? Not so much. That was not the last story of such things. Grandpa Doc was a passionate pioneer, courageous and wholehearted in his pursuits, and while inheriting his bravery, zeal and commitment for doing what is right, I had yet to learn his patience, prudence and timing. Gaining this kind of wisdom has always been a work in progress for me.

In spite of my shortcomings, my own ability to succeed first as a paramedic, then as a nurse in the shadow of this amazing man was in large part because I had the drive to push past my own limitations. As holds true for all of us, there were demons to conquer and lessons to learn. I thrived in the demanding, fast-paced world of emergency and intensive care medicine and loved the time spent in world-renowned hospitals and crazy "in the hood" emergency rooms of Southern California. These were the battlegrounds where I honed my skills and seemed to exist as a "warrior nurse," engaged in the conflicts and challenges of providing quality care. Grandpa Doc has been my touchstone, my reminder to be in service to others *and* to be good at what I did. He was the embodiment of strength I came back to when life seemed to be just too hard and who I shared my triumphs with. One of the proudest moments in my life was being the graduate to deliver a speech at our nursing pinning ceremony and seeing my grandfather in the front row, beaming at me with pride. I did not realize it at the time, but the bar had been set.

I had witnessed excellence in practice and I would always hold myself accountable to the standards of Grandpa Doc.

Take a moment to again consider what sort of things you imagined this path would provide you. Was there a person of influence? What was it that you admired about them? Considering these questions can help us be clear about our drives, hopes and dreams. Knowing what those are can help us correct our course, help us understand the bar we judge ourselves by and open our eyes to a clearer vision of what we want to create in our lives.

When We Become Disenchanted With It All

Thwarted idealism is often at the root of human discontent. For me, I wanted to be just like Grandpa. I felt such disappointment when in spite of my success, I still had so many struggles—both internally with my self-confidence and externally in my interpersonal relationships. I was judgmental and often became indignant when I thought others were not offering their best or when witnessing power struggles or ego taking precedence over doing what I believed was right for the patient. I felt frustration that so many caregivers were unhappy in their jobs—the irony being that I was unhappy in my job "because of them"! I spoke out, tried to advocate for better care, conditions, equipment, etc., but that often resulted in greater frustration for me and for others who were exposed to my self-righteous indignation and prideful self-importance. This was not exactly Grandpa Doc's style. Inevitably this approach always gave way, no matter how many ways I pitched it, to my burnout and feelings of hopelessness that things would never change. I would tell myself that I was "a square peg in a sea of round holes"...perhaps you can relate to such a feeling.

Back then I had little awareness of my part in creating the life I was experiencing and how I was getting in my own way. How could I possibly be a part of the problem when I strove to offer my best and always sought a high level of performance? I, like most folks, blamed circumstances and people for my dissatisfaction, burnout and failures. Eventually, thank God, I had the courage to dig in deeper and began to gain some insight through some professionally guided personal development work, books and seeking out the wise counsel of those I admired. I began to make some shifts to be more deliberate and conscious in creating the life I wanted. That effort has significantly altered the last two decades of my life and career. This is the journey I want to share with you.

I'm Glad To Have You Along

I suspect you are reading this book because you are, as I continue to be, in pursuit of something more. In the world of medicine, caring for people has always been viewed as noble, but it is also one of the hardest jobs there is. It is taxing physically, intellectually and emotionally. It is hard simply because what we do and the interactions we have, all have potential for significant consequences. "We are not," as a boss of mine liked to say, "flipping burgers here." Our version of forgetting to put extra pickles on the burger has the potential to drastically alter or even end the life of another human being. It is no small matter to survive, thrive and excel here.

No matter what your reasons for reading this book, whether you're a nurse, student, secretary, doctor, athlete, businessperson or some other type of achiever, I think you'll find some useful perspectives and new habits to incorporate that will help create more of what you want. This book is intended to open you to new possibility, lighten your heart and empower you to create the life and career you dream of. Like me, you may even become aware of how you've been standing in your own way.

If you haven't guessed it already, this will not be an academic read with references cited for each concept. Consider it more as a conversation with a friend or colleague who knows a bit of your world and the challenges therein, a person who's explored our humanness through a deep-dive into my own and has perspectives for you to consider.

It is also a book that I recommend be read at a leisurely pace. There's a lot to digest and reading it straight through, even on my own proof reads, is a bit much. Perhaps a chapter a week is a good strategy, that way you can think on things for a while and see how they may fit in your own life. You may even read chapters out of order, picking those that seem to fit your current focus. You may even pick it up a year later for a bit of inspiration and be surprised with new insights, because you have grown and changed. There are no rules here; you decide how to have this adventure.

My hope is that you'll find the content thought provoking and personal-reflection-inducing. You may even be a bit uncomfortable, as I am at times, when the content forces a bit of honesty with yourself about how you are going about life. Be patient, kind and forgiving with yourself as you make any needed adjustments. This is a personal journey—both the telling of my own, and yours as you read.

Happiness, I believe, is created by living fully in our gifts, talents and abilities, coupled with heartfelt efforts to help others discover theirs. Everyone's purpose is to discover, define and own what our gifts are and to consistently offer those to the best of our ability. This is how we develop our own brand of excellence and how we make our lives exceptional and satisfying. Finding those gifts is your unique quest, very specific to you, not what others define for you. Not all of us will become famous, rich or a celebrated talent, but it is important to note that our humble existence, when lived with such purpose, makes a difference in the grand scheme of things just the same.

"Tell me, what are you going to do with your one wild and precious life?"

Mary Oliver

··· 2 ···

The Investment Of You, Our Notions Of Excellence And Success

"Today you are You, that is truer than true. There is no one alive who is Youer than You."

Dr. Seuss, *Cat In The Hat*

MANY WILL HEAVE a sigh when asked to expend a bit of extra effort and question why they should invest the time to craft a personal brand of excellence. Many just want to go to work, meet the mandate, have no hassles, collect a check and put their energies into family, hobbies and the TV remote. We can do that and some happiness will be ours, but will we feel truly satisfied and successful?

I would have you consider for a moment, what is the most valuable asset we possess? OURSELVES of course...doesn't it make sense to grow that asset, just like we do our retirement funds? Do we really want to settle for a modest return? Just going through the motions of life or a job is such wasted opportunity. Doing so will never truly satisfy us or provide the greatest returns. After all, we spend a lot of time working, so wouldn't we want to make the best of it? Pursuing our own excellence, making the most of whatever we have to create a better self is one of the shrewdest investments we can make because of the simple fact that we are the one common denominator that all of our life pivots on.

Investing in ourselves requires no special circumstance. We don't need to wait until we get the right job, enough money, a good partner, or whatever we tell ourselves has to happen first. We can begin where we are. Our lives may be fairly complete and content, so maybe we just want to put a little extra shine on it. Our lives may be a hot mess. No matter. Whatever your story, just begin where you are.

We often believe excellence applies only to visible achievements, and that growing personally only happens in our favorite reading chair, a therapist's office or at a seminar. The truth is that any place and circumstance can hold opportunity for more and better. Ask yourself this: if I am spending X number of hours a day at my job, how can I make that X number of hours pay off in ways other than a paycheck? Or, how can I make a task that I'm dreading be a positive experience instead? EVERY job or experience has the potential to be more than its face value and can be time well spent. There is always something to glean, no matter the what or where.

How about these questions: Are my activities outside of work contributing positively to me? Are my friends the kind that help me grow or do they hold me back? All of it matters you see, because all elements of life are inextricably connected. Whatever our experience in one will inevitably bleed over to others. True success and happiness come when all elements of life are nurtured, where the good fruits of one can feed another. Collectively these elements create our futures and happiness, or if neglected they prevent us from achieving them.

The "investment of you" promises returns. There are many ways to invest—just look at the list of chapter titles and you can see that the ways are more than a few, each with its own special attribute to enhance your life. So let's get to it and explore how personal excellence is the common thread that pulls it all together.

Our Notions Of Excellence

We all have ideas about what excellence is, and we often think that it is something we can only hope to achieve in isolated circumstances, not something that can be applied pervasively in life. It was Martha Beck, a renowned sociologist and author, who said, "The way we do anything is the way we do everything." I believe what Ms. Beck is saying is that nothing in our lives happens in a silo. Everything is connected. No matter how subtle an act, thought or perception may seem to be, they all relate to one another in some way. When we do some things half-heartedly and others with best-effort gusto, the areas lacking that enthusiasm will always gnaw at us.

We can mistake the meaning of excellence. Does it mean perfection? How do our "notions of excellence" influence our lives and affect our willingness to take risks? Could our own beliefs about excellence be holding us back? Such beliefs unconsciously become the architects of our lives, shaping life to our benefit or detriment.

I remember a job, about eight years into my career, where I was working in a large emergency department. I had risen to being a charge nurse, but what I really wanted was to be a flight nurse. I knew I needed to get some experience in the intensive care units of a trauma and cardiac center, but the thought of leaving what I was so familiar with, had status in, and was good at, scared me. Leaving also introduced the possibility of failure. That fear not only delayed my dream, the lack of courage to go for it subtly evolved into resentment toward the job I had and affected my performance of it. That whole dynamic rippled through my life as well because I was beginning to adopt the habit of choosing what was safe, instead of what I aspired to. This story may sound familiar to some of you. I think we often hold ourselves back, worried about our ability to excel and achieve. I think doing so is a result of how we consciously or unconsciously think about excellence and how we perceive failure.

Many of us would say that excellence means "something exceptional," "getting it right all of the time," "knowing exactly what you are doing" or "mastery of a task." While this may be correct in part, is that the entire definition of excellence? How about the novice? Where does that leave them when they are striving for excellence and just learning about whatever it is that they are trying to master? Are we all excluded from excellence until we achieve mastery? How many "masters" of their craft, whatever it is that they excel at, have lost the joy of doing what they do so well? Are they still achieving excellence?

Excellence, if you look it up in the dictionary, often reflects something mostly to do with outcome or consistently exceeding the bar; "Unusually good and so surpasses ordinary standards" says Webster's. With this definition of excellence, we seem to focus on a "somewhere beyond" standard that is achievable by only a chosen few. It is no wonder we accept mediocrity as being adequate because excellence can seem out of reach for the average Joe. We can be riddled with doubt about our own ability to ever "be enough" so we don't even try to excel, leaving us to feel bereft and dissatisfied, just going through the motions to survive.

It is also curious that we can observe the amazing lives of those we think of as excellent, and fail to integrate the fact that none of them are successful all the time. The truly successful will tell you they have had heaps of so-called "failures." The curious part is, even when we cognitively get this, we *still* hesitate to try. Looking at their shining results, we just can't imagine how to get there ourselves or how we would survive in the event of failures.

Excellence and Perseverance

What is remarkable about all practitioners who have found their groove in excellence is that they maintain forward motion.

They stay focused on the goal and are deeply invested in learning from their so-called failures, honing their skills through this newfound knowledge because they view them as lessons. The expansion of knowledge, salvaged from the failure, is the "how" of their success—expanding instead of contracting as a result. They spend no time in disappointment or shame; they accept, gather up the lesson, and move on.

Vince Lombardi said in his first team meeting with the Green Bay Packers: "Gentlemen, we will chase perfection, and we will chase it relentlessly, knowing all the while we can never attain it. But along the away, we shall catch excellence." From that initial spark, the Packers cultivated a mentality that earned them five NFL championships and two Super Bowl wins in seven years. It was the perseverance and discipline to chase that elusive perfection that rewarded them with success.

Doing Things Perfectly Is A Myth

Somehow we've gotten the idea that excellence and excelling are synonymous with perfect or exceptional results. It's an all-or-nothing, or has-to-be-100%-right-or-it's-not-worth-much kind of approach. We focus on what's lacking instead of the effort put forth and whatever was gained or was achieved. We even hesitate to call something excellent if it has any perceived imperfection, (and if we can't see the imperfection, we will get busy trying to find one!) Because of this tendency to believe excellence is more rare than common, and our bent to "find the flaw" in ourselves, others, situations and things, many of us have given up the desire to excel and become cynical about putting forth this kind of effort. This in effect does make it more rare than common because we resign ourselves to mediocrity, assuring ourselves that most everything is flawed, therefore excellence can't really exist—at least in our personal world. This under-the-radar-never-risking-anything strategy also affords us some escape from outside scrutiny and can feel like a much safer alternative.

Our penchant to reserve excellence praise for only the "above and beyond" has also bred a culture of perfectionism. We want to be that perfect model of whatever it is that we do, yet resist the fact that imperfect humanness will eventually prevail, to some degree, with everyone. Because of this, many (dare I say most of us?) become unnerved when anything personal to us is pointed out as having flaws. We defend, make excuses, feel embarrassed, all because there is some form of perfectionism in our psyche. The more we resist or deny flaws in ourselves, the more inauthentic we become. A subtle anxiety builds as we scramble to project the image of perfection that we know, at least subconsciously, can never really exist.

Carol Dweck, a Stanford psychologist, has made it her life's work to research this obsession with perfection. What she has observed and verified is remarkably insightful, and she believes it originates with how we reward our children. In her work she identifies people as having either a "fixed" or "growth mindset." One or the other is cultivated in childhood and carried forward to adult perceptions and behaviors. We will explore her work in greater depth later, but which mindset we habitually use has been shown to be a very real and large predictor of our personal success and happiness.

I came from the place that Dweck describes as a fixed mindset, I've personally struggled to accept my imperfections and mistakes. When I'm not in acceptance, the lameness of my excuses ultimately becomes a greater humiliation and gives me more distress than having the flaw or making the mistake in the first place. Others instinctually do not admire or trust those who won't own their humanness, and we hamper our ability to improve if we fail to accept that effort to improve will include elements of failure. It is part and parcel of a human's endeavor to make progress.

The insistence on being perfect also promotes a culture where we don't report our mistakes. Under reporting of errors has been well documented in the medical world. It is easy to see why with the potential professional consequences and threat of suit. Our commitment and need to always get it right is appropriate, but not 100% achievable so long as the human element is involved.

Perfectionism also results in a competitive dynamic—and I don't mean in a good way. If you notice gossiping, intolerance for personality styles, a frequency of unkind or derogatory commentary about others in your workplace or social group, these would be signs of the unhealthy competitive dynamic I'm referring to. "OMG, did you hear about how Jean messed up?" or, "John is so irritating, yesterday he..." are examples of commentary found in such environments. Our subconscious obsession with perfection results in habitually being overly critical of mistakes and an unwillingness to accept individuality that doesn't match our vision of "perfect." We allow only those we are comfortable with to peacefully exist, the rest get our complaints. We may not always make comments out loud, but the thoughts in our head may live in a state of judgement just the same. Sadly, the root of it all lies in our own fear of being "found out" as something less than flawless because of this subtle belief that "perfect" is the only acceptable descriptor. Our comparisons, competitiveness and criticisms are all efforts to appear acceptable or better than others. I can't help but think of something my father used to say; "Don't cut off someone else's head so you can appear taller."

How Dare You Try To Rise Above!

Something else I have observed getting in the way of excelling is how others can react to it. Some may think that an individual's effort to excel is an act of arrogance. We ourselves may even worry about excelling because it might make others "feel bad" if we achieve and they don't. With this misguided rationale about how to preserve our relationships, we sometimes don't try because we want others to be comfortable. While that may be considered sweet, humble and/or kind, is that really where we want to be when considering the greater good? Marianne Williamson made the wise observation, "We ask ourselves, who am I to be brilliant, gorgeous, talented and fabulous? Actually, who are you not to be?...There is nothing enlightened about shrinking so that other people won't feel insecure about you... As we let our own Light shine, we unconsciously give other people permission to do the same."

It is through our examples of effort and achievement that we can inspire others to grow, achieve, explore, invent and reinvent. Including others in our achievements, encouraging others to seek their own successes and letting them see our own vulnerabilities and struggles as we attempt to achieve, can illuminate possibilities and encourage unlimited growth and success.

In the more competitive climates, we can also lose our ability to genuinely celebrate the success of others. When we are overly competitive we can become so self-focused that if something isn't celebrating us, we get uncomfortable, feeling "less than" or somehow deficient. This narcissistic viewpoint can have us believing the success of another is some kind of spotlight focused on our own shortcomings, leaving us jealous, insecure, and envious. I have caught myself thinking in the midst of a colleague's recognition, "Why am I not getting the recognition, after all I have done that and better!" We seem to have a need to constantly compare and judge ourselves as worthy and doing so brings up a parade of anxieties about not being enough.

Though well intended, we even project this worry on our children in a misguided attempt to make life easier for them. In our effort to have our children "feel good," we have decided that everyone in Little League or dance class needs a trophy. Doing so places feelings above personal effort and accomplishment. Without effort and challenges, the obtainment of a goal or getting a trophy lacks meaning.

It also registers in a child's mind that they *should* get recognition and reward, regardless of effort or performance. Do you think this has contributed greatly to the sense of entitlement and lack of ambition that is so troubling today? I do. This "everybody is a star" philosophy gives the underlying impression that being singled out as exceptional, standing out among the crowd or being acknowledged for something earned is a negative, is embarrassing or demeaning to others, or somehow elitist. I also suspect that eventually these children realize they have been fraudulently rewarded and their insecurities grow to even greater proportions because of it. Perhaps the worst fallout of this approach is that we rob our children of learning to be gracious with admiration for the winner, learning to be resilient in the face of failure, and learning that they don't always need to be the center of attention.

Excellence Is A State Of Being

Consider for a moment that nothing has ever been done perfectly, meaning as good as it could possibly ever be. If that were true, there would be no evolution, no next, newest, greatest thing. It really is time for our misguided views of excellence to be reworked in how we think about it.

Excellence always has a place to manifest in our lives and is less dependent on outcome than you think. As a colleague once said to me when I asked him what he thought excellence was; "Excellence is a state of being...something you choose to be, not necessarily something you accomplish through a task." He was speaking to the questions of where is our focus? What are our guiding principles? Is our integrity alive and well, guiding what we do? It is that *underlying state of being* that makes the difference between getting something done and doing something well, because whatever state of being we chose infiltrates what we do. When our state of being is truly focused on personal excellence, we generate a passion for the doing and end up doing it to the best of our ability. Wikipedia is on to something in their secondary description of excellence as it takes into account the evolving nature of things and the need for adaptability: "Excellence is a continuously moving target that can be

25

pursued through actions of integrity...meeting all obligations and continually learning and improving in all spheres to pursue the moving target." Having a state of being that understands this gives us an advantage; a willingness to be malleable and change ourselves or our approach in order to excel and do what needs to be done. It is a hallmark in the lives of many great men and women.

Traits, talents, attitudes, effort, core values, habits and behaviors all play a part in finding our own personal sweet-spot in life. Some of these come naturally, others we have to work at. No one is gifted with the total package from the start. Having the courage to honestly evaluate who we are, how we think and where our strengths and weaknesses lie is how we catapult ourselves to more and better. Sometimes that can be a bit unnerving because we may not like what we find on close inspection, but trust me, you'll survive, and you'll like yourself even more for making the effort and having the guts to do it honestly.

Share The Wealth

It is important to understand that excellence is at the height of its power when it is shared through its *interdependent* creation. While outcomes for patients are at the forefront of every excellent practitioner's agenda, the underpinnings of creating those outcomes largely depend on our various relationships and interactions with others. Creating excellence in our practice will never be fully achieved until excellence in our teams and relationships also exists. It is not possible to create the life-changing satisfying results I am speaking of if we are only operating in an independent silo. Bringing others with us on that journey is critical because how we influence our environment and those around us is an important piece of feeling satisfied with who we are and our influence in the world. Creating excellence synergistically is infinitely more satisfying and can create success beyond what we've imagined.

Exceling In The Work World

Mike Dooley, a motivational speaker and author, explained that in order to manifest a better life experience, it is a simple matter of "Doing all you can, with all you've got, from where you are." The right set of circumstances is not required. That does not mean that we shouldn't try to create the right set of circumstances to succeed, but we all know that the best laid plans can be thwarted and at times we have to proceed as best we can.

Having employees, or being the kind of employee, who makes the effort to contribute to a functionally healthy and satisfying work environment are the true gold of any organization, regardless of their status as novice or expert, as an organizational leader, working professional or vocational member of that group. Organizations aren't expecting everyone to be an expert, but they do want everyone to practice excellence by putting forth their best. Organizations become transformative when every employee—from the CEO down to the frontline employees—is supported to "Do all they can, with what they've got, from where they are" to achieve the organizational mission. Such environments foster people to excel and individuals are bolstered by their own sense of contribution. What follows is a sense of well-being, individual pride and a sense of team emerges as personal relationships strengthen as a result of everyone practicing this principle. We are also wise to remember that this prevailing attitude and habit of "all we can" is applied to big *and* little things. All of it matters. Striving for as close to perfect as we can get and acknowledging both others and ourselves for this kind of effort is how we synergistically create more and better results, both personally and in team efforts.

Part of the challenge to doing our best is having our own intrinsic motivation. Our employers ask for our excellence but, being human, they may lose sight of when habitual excellence exists and fail to voice their appreciation for our efforts. Any employer paying us to do a job has the reasonable expectation that we will do our best while on their clock. Just showing up is not enough for them or for you. But expecting and requiring external validation as your motivator will never sustain you or even be possible. Employers do themselves a favor when they recognize their people, but having to have it in order to put forth effort on our part is a lose-lose proposition. Creating our own internal motivation we'll explore in depth later, and the cultivation of truly intrinsic motivators that last a lifetime are a large part of what make us truly happy.

Finding the sweet-spot is more than just the application of our talents. In any given situation—at work, at home or in the world—it can boil down to asking the simple question; "What can I do at this moment to improve the current situation?" It could be as simple as cleaning the counter, picking up some trash, listening to someone, smiling at someone or rubbing the shoulders of an over-taxed loved one. It could be taking the opportunity to teach or help someone improve their skills. It could even be taking a minute to look for a reason to compliment someone, encourage or make them laugh. These large and small acts are the kind of things that make up a life that is satisfying, sweet and make the world a better place one bit at a time.

Just as educators outline a curricula so that we have the nuts and bolts of what we wish to accomplish, I thought it useful to break down all the bits of what creates a sweet spot, a happy life and good relationships. We don't get a lot of this kind of ongoing education once we leave our family of origin. I actually shudder at the number of years I lived my life without a conscious effort to understand and employ some of the elements we'll get into. In all honesty it usually took a painful experience to motivate me to any sort of questioning about how I was doing things.

I'm also increasingly aware that growing up in our current society may have us at a serious deficit when it comes to teaching our younger generations. In my opinion, we have relinquished much of the responsibilities to other sources like our schools and relentless social media sources. More and more data is coming out that this has been costly, with greater numbers of suicides, substance abuse and a declining overall sense of happiness.

Nothing can effectively replace the experience of sitting around the dinner table hearing about everyone's day and receiving the wisdom of our elders. In fact, many have all but discarded our elderly as a burden and irrelevant. What happened to our culture that had reverence and respect for life experience? We've forgotten that elders can provide insight, give us a sense of belonging and nurture us through the exchange of love.

Life is jam-packed with distraction. The list of things we participate in that don't really add happiness value is long. It's up to us to choose activities wisely. It is up to us to manage our internal environments when things are challenging. There is much to consider in the following chapters, so take your time. Take what resonates with you and enjoy the benefits of creating—deliberately—a life that is joyous, fulfilling and unique to you. So let's get crackin'.

UNDERPINNINGS

••• 3 •••

Humor, Joy And Faking It Until You Make It

"There is no greater panacea for sorrow, no better reviving tonic, and no greater beauty than a genuine smile."

Paramahansa Yogananda

HAVE YOU EVER had the experience of leaving work with your face hurting because you have laughed and smiled so much? What a revelation.

Humor is one of the simplest and often underrated tools we have to cultivate happiness, even in the face of gravity. It's a good thing there is constant fodder all around us for lightening up! I put humor in the first position of happy life tools because it sometimes is the only thing we can do to improve a given situation.

In the world of combat, heathcare, law enforcement and EMS, we are known for our dark humor. It clearly is a coping mechanism for what is faced on a daily basis and making each other laugh is one of the ways we handle the stress and heal the wounds that come when wrestling with life in these forums. It can be somewhat shocking to those who don't work in that environment, but laughter is one of those things that can shake you awake to resourcefulness when stuck. It loosens the grip of stress and lightens what feels heavy, making us more capable of letting go of elements we cannot control. It also interrupts the storing of frightening experiences in long term memory.

There are tricks to humor. One being not to make it at the expense of others. Anything catty or meanspirited doesn't elevate the vibe at all. Now that doesn't mean that we can't make fun of ourselves. In fact self-deprecating humor is a gift that helps others lighten up and let go of that "have to be perfect" mentality. Another trick for humor is to not be overly sensitive. I mean really...getting a chuckle out of my own humanness provides me with a lot of material. In fact, I like to say that life is just a series of pauses between nerdly acts! I find I also cut other people a lot more slack when I am able to laugh at my own goofiness and misfires.

I do worry sometimes about our high focus on "being sensitive." I have noticed that more and more people seem to have a default of being offended and somewhat incapable of seeing irony, or taking a second to see how the circumstances they are in IS funny given how you could not even make it up. In my house we have a saying, "Life can be described in two ways: A really good time, or a really good story." We love it because it reminds us to lighten the heck up when challenges arise. I'm sure you yourself have told dozens of stories about stressful events that had everyone in stiches on the retelling of it.

I'm also sure you have friends that you love spending time with because they are so stinkin' funny. Cultivate those humor relationships, tell them how much you enjoy their company because of their humor and they are likely to do it all the more. You will also have the added benefit of becoming more funny yourself as you observe your friend's wit and exercise your own neuropathways of humor.

The science of humor is also impressive. Feel-good endorphins are something humans crave and are released with laughter. Even a *forced smile* releases bits of endorphins in most humans and more often than not evolves into a genuine smile releasing endorphins in greater quantities. Laughter is also associated with better digestion, a sense of underlying and lasting joy/well-being and our overall job satisfaction. It has the ability to lower blood pressure and enhance healing. Why would anyone want to resist the opportunity to deploy humor?

I admit there have been times I find myself humorless, taking things a little too seriously. While there are plenty of times requiring solemn and thoughtful consideration, it can become an unbalanced, habitual way of viewing the world and our circumstances. We NEED humor, from both a biological and psychological perspective. When it becomes hard to muster humor, just fake it 'til you make it! This is not an act of insincerity, it is simply the practice trying to find the humor and intentionally breaking the pattern of behavior or thought we are currently in. It's similar to taking your child for ice cream after just having left the Urgent Care for stitches, shifting focus and adding something pleasurable. The zero calorie version is to go pet a dog, watch a comedy, play with your kids or take in the vision of something beautiful to get your mind off topic. Imagine what your favorite comedian would say on the subject. Humor can be a transformative helper.

Well, let's soldier on to meatier subjects. This chapter may have been brief, but no less important than the rest. It's good to have had a visit to staying light-hearted as the next chapter requires a bit of seriousness...but remember to bring along your sense of humor!

··· 4 ···

The Foundational Nature of Integrity

"Let your life speak."

Parker J. Palmer

I HAVE HEARD it said, "If we understand our why, we can make it through any how." Our personal "why" for the life we are living is found in the core values we have formulated, whether we are aware of those values or not. They are actually foundational to how we experience life. The degree of peace in our lives depends on the harmony between the "how" we do it and those values, or "whys." Indeed our own brand of excellence and sweet-spot in life can never be wholly created, let alone satisfying, without a thorough examination and tuning of these to be in harmony, which is what I call our integrity. If there were one thing to have in order for a life of happiness, peace and success, it would be our personal integrity.

Our thoughts, words and deeds tell a story about who we are. My personal happiness and excelling in what I do were hugely enhanced when I came to understand the foundational nature of my integrity and began consciously shaping my life according to principles I valued. I know we all think we do this by default, but whether we do this with absolute integrity *and consciously* is worth exploring because it is so easy to fool ourselves. Integrity is a deeply personal thing. It takes wisdom and consideration for the whole of life to get down to the nitty-gritty of what really matters. It also may take fortitude to shake off outside influences of what we may feel pressured to accept. It takes courage to commit to what really matters to you and reject behaviors and opinions that don't stand the acid test of what you describe as valuable and acceptable.

Understand that it is unlikely that any of us think and act with integrity 100% of the time. I know that I miss the mark on occasion. We are human. We are constantly subjected to competing internal needs and wants in addition to demands from others and situations. Sometimes, our lesser selves will have us acting or thinking in ways that, in hindsight, don't really line up with our definition of our better selves—you know, those acts or thoughts that generate a sort of internal cringe when we've been in territory we don't admire. What is most important is that we endeavor to live consciously enough to avoid these stumbles with some consistency. When we become aware of failings on our part, we own the missteps, correct ourselves, consider how we got there and reset to that state we have committed ourselves to. This is how we do the right thing with consistency, even when other motivators tug at our humanness. It's a way of living that can take time to develop, but the practice of integrity becomes hardwired with practice.

Integrity is about getting honest about how we are living and aligning our course with where we really want to go. Doing so creates a true freedom and a sense of peace that all good people want for themselves, making it worth the investment of our time and effort. If you were to read only one chapter of this book and also complete the exercise in the back of the book, this alone has the potential to be the most life changing of all.

The truth about integrity as I have come to know it is this: any unrest or dis-ease we may experience arises because what we are thinking, doing or saying does not match what we know to be right, good and most valued. Do you wonder why so many people are experiencing more anxiety than ever before? I think it is from the fragmentation that occurs when how we are living doesn't match what we value. Events in the world also cause anxiety because what is occurring doesn't match what we value. While we often have little control over world events, we can address how we are personally living. Repairing this kind of fragmented existence is what heals less-than-satisfying lives. Doing so provides us with both ease and an exhilaration in the life we are living. We become free of guilt and it fuels a commitment to continually evolve for the better. The question you have to answer is, do you want to put in the work? It's not particularly difficult. It just demands a conscious commitment to stay in the saddle. Notice I did not say "get" in the saddle as you likely have already mounted up and embraced integrity to some degree. If your current feelings while reading this entail a sense of resistance, then for sure there is work to do because as I said, that discomfort you are feeling is your better self talking. So get your foot in that stirrup and let's ride.

Integrity's Nuts and Bolts

Just as steel rebar and cement are the foundation of any modern building, our integrity is the supportive structure underlying everything we do. If you ask someone what integrity is, they may have difficulty defining it. Many think that if their life is reasonably functional, pay their debts, etc., they must have integrity. I would argue that *how we experience life* is the most telling.

At its simplest, integrity means, "I am whole." It is a concept where there is consistency between our behaviors (our thoughts/words/deeds) and our beliefs. It is also about those behaviors being in alignment with what we want to achieve. Having integrity means that we strive to be without "fractures" or inconsistencies between what we believe in and want, and what we think, say and do. It is doing the right thing, whether anyone knows we did so or not.

There was a time in my life that I would vehemently argue that I had integrity because I could tell you what was right or wrong, and I made a point of keeping up appearances when it came to doing the right thing. My credit score was excellent, I had good friends and a growing career. Any variance from what I knew to be right I carefully kept under wraps...like spending money when I knew it was counter to agreements with my husband, or when I told a "little white lie" because it served some purpose. It was just a way of operating that seemed to be the normal way folks went about their business. I make good money, why can't I buy that leather jacket? Or I privately rationalized that my mistake wasn't a big deal. Or when leaving out critical details to make me look better, I would think, "Well, everyone does that, right?" While none of these were very egregious acts, they subtly ate at me. I had not taken full stock of how that kind of falseness was insidiously affecting my life and self-confidence. I had yet to dig deep enough to fully understand what living in integrity really meant.

The Relationship Between Integrity and Core Values

My own journey to satisfaction with life made huge advancements when I got clear about and committed to what my core values were. I realized I had never stopped long enough to fully digest what those values meant to me and to honestly evaluate if my thoughts, words and deeds consistently reflected them. I also was operating with some core values I no longer believed in but had simply become habitual ways of thinking. This was not a particularly easy process. I felt a bit embarrassed when I got honest about how I was doing some things, but challenging myself to bravely do so rewarded me handsomely. If you are feeling squeamish at this moment, or maybe trying to distance yourself in some way, know that it's a signal telling you there's still work to do!

This kind of evaluation is not about making ourselves wrong for how we have approached things up to this point. It's about awareness, setting a target and honing who we are to the best, most polished version of what we envision. We must be brave enough to challenge our own actions and willing to honestly assess, learn from and correct ourselves when warranted. The practice of integrity becomes easier with repetition. We can find pride in our improvement and let go of any shame we may feel for slipping-up.

Many would say that core values are what we were raised with, an immutable set that our cultural and family upbringing bestows on us. While that may be partially true, it is important to realize that values can evolve as we experience more. The world has many people who came from horrible upbringings, cultures of bigotry or injustice, or where they were taught to prey on the weakness of others, but who learned to choose differently when their values changed.

I know when I started this process, I was surprised to find that I was actually living a few degrees off of what I thought were my inherent values. I was a good and decent person, but I had rationalized and drifted. What I lacked was awareness that I had been influenced by cultural things that I didn't really believe in. I had failed to apply the discipline necessary to stay aligned with what I valued. Virtues like patience, kindness and honesty I selectively applied to fit my moods, motives or how I felt about a person. During my employment as a logistics manager for self-improvement group forums where I heard from and observed hundreds of people doing this kind of work, I learned that the same "drift" was surprisingly common among people—highly successful people, people in positions of power and just regular folks. My heretofore unrecognized duress over living this way, was a common human experience.

Roles and Core Values

Other changes in core values occur as our circumstances morph. When I was single and without children, my life principles did not have much focus on kids and committed relationships. When I met my husband, being wholly committed and faithful arrived as a sacred core value, along with nurturing our son. As our depth of understanding and life experience expands, so do the things we value.

In our caregiver roles, what do we consider most important? What and how does our "ideal" healthcare practitioner, (father, mother, CEO or whatever roles you play) say, act, and think? What would our patient, colleague, child or employee need most from us to truly thrive? Answering these questions produces the list of core values that benefit us and those around us. Listing such things is how mission statements are developed and personal excellence and associated happiness requires the same sort of appraisal. Consider also that values are not limited to just those in our inner circle. Values are meant to be evident in a way that fosters everyone's well-being.

Living our core values and life principles is not a one-time weekend project. It would be nice if it were that easy, but in the context of our daily learning and a rapidly changing world, it entails recurrent and honest self-evaluation and the self-discipline to correct our course when necessary. When we sign up for wanting more out of our lives we have to habitually ask, especially when difficulties arise, self-reflecting questions such as, "What was I really after in that interaction? Serving my ego or serving another person?" or, "Did I act in a way that I can be proud of?" and "Did I act in accordance with what I value most? Will behaving and thinking that way get me more of what I really want?"

So Where Are You At? An Exercise For Clarity

You've probably already thought about a few core values during our discussion that you already hold dear. If you have never done a pen-to-paper core values assessment or have not done so recently, the exercise I mentioned in the back of this book is worth doing. It's the only exercise in this book and it is the most valuable one I can offer. My website, cjsnow.net, has others that are useful for various things that challenge us in life, but I wanted this one readily accessible and waiting for you. Even if you have done a similar exercise before, doing it again now may surprise you. Your clarity will likely increase since the last time you did it. It's a practice I have incorporated with some degree of frequency and have found hugely valuable in keeping me on track.

The initial portion of the exercise takes about twenty to thirty minutes, so make sure you have the private time to complete the initial steps. It is done privately so only you are involved. The full exercise is conducted over several weeks as you practice in your daily life. The exercise is critical in ferreting out the subtle fractures in our integrity. A simple example of an integrity fracture is having a core value of being respectful to others, yet because we find ourselves feeling irritable we end up barking unpleasantly at someone we may not consider consequential in our world, like a grocery clerk. Or, we may say that honesty is a core value, yet we fail to step up and take ownership of an error we made. We tell ourselves these are small matters, while our conscience notices and secretly cannot forgive, giving us that feeling of dis-ease. I think you will be missing something truly valuable if you skip the actual "doing" part of this exercise, so I hope you will check it out. It takes some courage to do so, but I believe you have it in you to look honestly in the mirror and as you continue reading you'll get even more ideas of how to make this useful.

I now know, with zero doubt, that if I have feelings of angst or being out of sorts or am experiencing a less than satisfying life, then somewhere in the scheme of things what I value and what I'm thinking, doing or saying, are not aligned, so I get busy correcting my course, which often begins with some type of integrity check. It has been such a life changing thing to do that I often return to this kind of reflection whenever life seems amiss.

Examples In Life Experience Of How This Works

In my practice as a nurse, I have a clear core value of "...*in every situation, do what is right for the patient.*" I have affirmed this for so many years in my practice that it is now second nature, even if it is uncomfortable and I have to question a grouchy colleague about an order, or risk showing ignorance about something, or perhaps I have to do some other uncomfortable task. It has become my predominant habit to correct hesitation and do all the above willingly because I am aligned with my responsibility to *advocate and care for my patient*. At home, it may be uncomfortable to sincerely apologize and admit to my husband that I was wrong about something, but I value *honest relationships* and *taking ownership of my actions* so I take the leap. Though not always easy to do, making the apology gives me ease because I am realigning my actions with my core values.

In the above examples, stepping into and aligning with our core values does not easily happen every time for any of us. Things like fear or pride can get in the way. In the course of con-tinually practicing to live life aligned with what I value most, my missteps become fewer and farther between and the subse-quent pride in having corrected my course becomes a stronger motivator than the shame of acknowledging I was off track. The more we practice, the more consistent we become, the fewer regrets we have.

I want to reiterate here: This kind of evaluation is not about making ourselves wrong for how we have approached things in the past. It's about awareness, setting a target and honing who we are to the best, most polished version of what we envi-sion. True, deep and committed integrity is kept alive this way and enhances how we experience life. Like any skill, the prac-tice of it becomes easier with repetition. We can find pride in our improvement and let go of any shame we may feel for slipping-up.

The more we commit to staying aligned, the fewer messes we make and the easier it becomes to clean them up when we do take a misstep. We learn to gracefully apologize or correct the error because being aligned with our values becomes more important than the embarrassment of admitting to a mistake. Ownership of our actions gradually feels more comfortable and seems sensible with practice, rather than a shameful experience. It is something akin to scrubbing out a dirty wound so that it may heal properly—a bearable discomfort. As our self-correction becomes easier, a sense of pride begins to emerge and we regain a sense of wholeness, knowing we have done our best to live with true integrity. The self-respect and the chance for healing with others is enhanced by these humble acts and we become more respected by others for doing so.

Sometimes Stuck Between A Rock And A Hard Place

In professional life, there may be times our roles mandate we do something that doesn't quite jive with our values, situations where we are not in full control of what goes on. There will always be factors and things we cannot change and most of us have hierarchies we have to live in. These factors can create what feels like "a rock and hard place" where the available choices aren't what we believe to be optimal or the right thing to do. In nursing, we may, in fact, be obligated to carry out an order that we do not agree is the right course of action. In my case, my employer expected me to support a patient's heavy medication regimen which is counter to my core value of maintaining health in a more holistic way. How are we to say our personal integrity is intact under these circumstances?

It comes down to asking ourselves if we have done everything we can to affect the outcome. Moral duress, that dis-ease I mentioned earlier, follows us if we fail to speak up and advocate for what we believe is right or fail to consider all the avenues we have to effect change. Many of us choose not to act because we fear that "making waves" will have consequences. Sometimes they do, and some consequences are worth bearing, for a greater good is at stake. Other times we have to simply resign ourselves to the fact that there is nothing we can do. Sometimes, we may even choose to leave a set of circumstances because it is so far out of alignment with what we value.

Integrity means that we exercise our power and influence to do good whenever we can. Let's say a doctor's order I am given seems counter to what my experience tells me is the right course of action. Do I share those thoughts with the doc or ask some questions? As for the patient on multiple medications, I can inquire if they have interest in information about augmenting their health with more holistic approaches such as diet, lifestyle or exercise. I can also encourage their exploration of the growing practice of Integrative or Holistic medicine if they are so inclined. These are examples of what we can do, but a degree of acceptance of what happens from there is required.

When we chose not to act on something we feel strongly about, we may feel a cowardice that we secretly cannot bear. "Going along to get along" can have its consequences. We harbor it subconsciously, it eats at us, and as our integrity erodes through our own lack of action to influence where we can, so does our happiness, our confidence and our belief that we have the ability to live a life that is fulfilling.

Sometimes, despite our acts of courage, what we think should have happened, doesn't. We can feel disheartened by this, but at the end of the day, what mattered is that we made efforts where we could, which preserves the integrity between our values and behaviors. In medicine, most of us have experienced patient outcomes that are distressing because something was missed or a mistake made. The best we can do here is advocate for learning and safety measures so that such outcomes are avoided. This is not about assigning blame, it about learning.

Operating in the confines of hierarchy of an imperfect world requires an ability to accept its imperfections. Grasping this and comprehending what we cannot control, and controlling what we can, is what will keep us loving what we do and at peace with our part in it. If we cannot hold this perspective, cynicism and unhappiness generally follow.

Keeping Our Word

Keeping our word and meaning what we say, how much does it really matter? Integrity in communication demands that we be thoughtful about what we say and what we commit to. This is twofold: 1) we stay committed to what we said we would do long after the mood we said it in has left us, and; 2) we communicate with others in authentic ways that match our core values. Too often we agree to do things without a real intention to commit to them and too often our conversations lack thought and sincerity.

It seems to me that we have largely become a society of empty promises, unfulfilled commitments and patronizing "yeses" when what people would rather say is "no." The scariest part is that we are getting lulled into this being a norm and fail to realize the price we pay for just accepting it as so. If asked, most of us would say that we believe our word should mean something and that keeping it is valuable. It should be no surprise then, that being lax about keeping our word or communicating in inauthentic ways are other means by which our "wholeness" erodes.

I believe that most people commit to things with the best of intentions and a desire to please, but fail to give much thought as to how practical or even possible it may be to honor the commitment. If we are the type of person who gives many agreeable responses just because we want to be agreeable, we may eventually find ourselves completely exhausted by our efforts to please. We may earn a bad reputation because our follow-through is poor, and this erodes our comfort and satisfaction with life.

It has taken me a long time to understand and accept that I cannot be everything to everyone. Even though my input may be requested on many projects and I have a compulsion to be a contributor, some of my unhappiest times are when I feel the pressures of being over-committed and have a calendar so full that I don't have time to breathe. Being busy and highly productive is how I like my life to be, but it can also be a runaway horse.

Getting ahead in many workplace cultures seem to demand that we kill ourselves in the process if we are to be deemed worthy of advancement. It is a fine balance to be earnest and hardworking while preserving our sanity. We have a ways to go in learning that in our workplaces. In my own experience, I have almost always found that to be true when in positions of leadership and I believe the reason why so many clearly talented people won't step up into such positions.

Not completing what we promised is a bitter pill to swallow. So here's the hard part...we have to learn to be thoughtful and say "no" with some wisdom. If, instead, we say "yes" we must be disciplined enough to bear the burden of fulfilling the commitment, even if it becomes inconvenient or painful to do so. Others may be disappointed with the "no"—and we may miss that momentary satisfaction of pleasing someone else—but it gets easier with time as we get clear about priorities. It is far better to say, "I'll think about it" and later say yes or no when we have arrived at a decision, or communicate that our plate is full and that some things may need to be reprioritized. It is poor form to say yes and have our primary priorities suffer in the process of fulfilling the obligation. We can even become resentful, blaming the commitment or organization for "sucking us dry" instead of owning the fact that we were thoughtless in our saying yes. We have to thoughtfully advocate for a workplace that supports the health of its people. Unbalanced, overly demanding workplace cultures will never change if we don't hold our ground, earn and advocate for better.

As we practice being fully aware of what kind of life we are trying to create, it gets easier for us to say no. While we all should be ready to share our gifts, talents and abilities, it should not be at the expense of our own stability. If you are reading this book I would guess you are one of life's doers, someone who has a hard time saying no, someone driven to step up and act. Our challenge is to inspire more doers, to help others find their own gifts, talents and abilities instead of staying stuck in thinking that we have to do all the doing.

I am still a work in progress on the subject of saying no. I generally have such enthusiasm and so many ideas that I often feel I am drowning in them. I can get involved in so many personal and professional pursuits that I feel overwhelmed and out of balance. Because of this there are times when I fail to deliver in a timely fashion. Understanding how I get myself there, handling my desire to please and accomplish, are all components that I am still learning to manage. When I am thoughtful about my commitments, I do better. I am learning to encourage others to step up and contribute rather than thinking it has to be me who carries out every task.

Authentic Communication

Meaning what we say and integrity in communication have other subtle distortions as well. Many forms of communication have become habituated. Take for example the routine question of "How are you?" You might be genuinely interested in the well-being of your best friend, but how about for the store clerk or coworker? As the question's receiver, do we usually say "Fine, and you?" without taking any inventory of how we really are doing or applying any real interest in this exchange? This of course does not mean that we disclose all our troubles each time we're asked, but it is a call to truly show some interest in the welfare of others and to have some awareness about how we, or others, are doing personally. Not every day is a great day. When we disclose a bit of our human experience, it serves as a reminder to do what we can to make it a better one, to offer help or words of encouragement to another or to interject some humor into life's challenges.

Developing authentic communication has the potential for creating highly effective relationships because we are afforded a clearer picture of what others are experiencing. It keeps us aware that we are operating in a world with multiple individual experiences and realities. Isn't it easier to work with someone when you have an idea about how they're really doing? It promotes understanding and can reduce the tendency to personalize how others interact with us. Knowing someone is having a hard time with something helps us to be aware of how we can contribute to improving circumstances, maybe cut them a little slack or help to shift their mood in some way. Trust builds when people know we care about them.

Some time ago there was a physician I really liked working with. I began to notice I was liking him a lot less because he was becoming abrupt and impatient. I thought I might have done something to offend him. So I gathered up the courage to ask him, "Are you OK, or have I done something to upset you? I've just noticed that you are really short with me and I value the kind of relationship we've had before." Much to my surprise, I learned he was undergoing a very painful divorce. Amid his profuse apologies he was close to tears. It was a risk to approach him, but the payoff was huge. I was better able to understand that at this point in his life, it was challenging for him to be at his best and I could stop personalizing his poor communication. He also appreciated the words of encouragement I offered, and so our mutual trust deepened when he understood that I valued and supported him at a time in his life when he was not feeling particularly valued and supported.

Not every such encounter, of course, will go that way as not everyone is willing to self-disclose. Some may even resent the question "How are you?" because the answer is so painful. But letting people know that we genuinely care about them can go a long way toward building bridges. Having the patience to continue offering support, even though their response to the simplest interaction may be less than you would hope for, is likely to eventually gain some traction and produce greater, more satisfying results.

Interacting in authentic ways to improve relationships can occasionally be a slower process then we might hope for. Sometimes people need time to digest, and then, seemingly out of the blue, things get better as though the other difficulties never happened. "Hmmmm...I'll take it!" we think as we silently celebrate the win. There may or may not be significant personal bonding, but trust begins to build and the possibility for more grows. Communication still is one of my biggest challenges, but my perseverance to communicate in authentic ways continues to yield results.

Our words also have a power that must be respected—they can uplift as easily as they can tear down. Validating others and offering safe forms of communication, even to those that are angry or holding a grudge, creates possibility for better relations. I have been amazed by how helpful that approach can be and surprised by positive results when I make an effort to first connect, and then attend to whatever lies between us. Admittedly there are some who, sadly, will "not budge from their grudge." That is a loss for both of us, but my job is to continue communicating with integrity, and I feel infinitely better for trying.

Lastly, our words and actions can authentically represent us or be a phony façade. In a world that so often judges our words, I sometimes find my words strangled as I attempt authentic communication. I know for sure just going along with conversations that don't represent who I am is an offense to my authentic self. Our conscience is always observing and will always judge us against our core values. We have to find a way to navigate our current strangled forms of communication and be able to hear and discuss views that don't match our own without the violence and anger that is becoming more common.

Our Built-in Barometer

Our general state of happiness and satisfaction with it all is a fabulous and acutely accurate barometer. If something feels "off," take an inventory as to why; was there an action, (or perhaps a lack of courageous action,) or a way of thinking that does not align with your core values? Are there things committed to but not fulfilled gnawing at you? Are you communicating with others in a way that is caring and genuine? Have you been neglecting things important to you? Dishonoring our word, maligned core values and being inauthentic in communication all have a price, the most palpable being our own contentment.

The Multitiered Effect of Broken Integrity

There are sometimes devastating effects for others outside the parties immediately involved when we choose to not stand in our integrity. The outward rippling effect of seemingly small transgressions in integrity have been responsible for ruining lives, careers, friendships, families, even nations. The price is often high, sometimes even tragic. How willing are we to say "It doesn't really matter" when we can have so little comprehension how our transgressions play out? It is so much better to be responsible and just not go there.

Worse yet, the more often we choose to let our integrity slip, the more it seems normal to do so. Soon, we can find ourselves operating habitually and thoughtlessly in that mode. Entire groups of people can be convinced that violating standards of integrity is acceptable when so many are doing it. This is how we can lose our way and perpetuate darkness in the world.

Stepping fully into our integrity, even when inconvenient, personally costly or unpopular, learning to keep our word consistently and meaning what we say is a daily practice that takes conscious living and watchful attention. I believe it is our primary duty if we have even a modest interest in being a good citizen wanting to affect the world positively. It is all too easy to fall back into old habits and misguided group think if we are not paying attention and assessing our progress or regression.

When we identify personal actions, thoughts or habits that do not fit what we believe or want to achieve, it takes courage to do something thoughtful to change them. Making necessary apologies, mustering up the nerve to address an issue, strategizing how to handle situations differently next time, walking in the world at large with our integrity intact—all of this puts us back in command of our lives and actively creating the life we want and are proud of. Having integrity brings us relief from the stressors of an inauthentic life. It brings us peace. Life becomes simpler and it perpetuates goodness in the world. It's not all that difficult to do when we cultivate and establish a habit of guardianship over our integrity.

••• 5 •••

A Sense Of Contribution

"When you cease to make a contribution, you begin to die."

Eleanor Roosevelt

MAINTAINING OUR INTEGRITY, excelling in the world and becoming satisfied with the life we are living is largely dependent on having a sense of contribution—a sense that we matter and can make a difference. I believe most people in healthcare understand this and that it was part of their motivation to enter into the field in the first place. It is a gift really to have this level of contribution built in to a career choice. One would think that having it would make it easier to sustain our level of satisfaction. But it doesn't always. There are a myriad of reasons why this is so which we will explore later. For now, let's look at the concept of "contribution."

Current research, as beautifully illustrated in Tom Schadyac's film *I Am,* reveals that we are—at the core of our DNA, no less—creatures of community. It's in our very nature to support and contribute to each other, whether we are biologically related or not. In ancient times, the concept of a "family unit" did not exist. The focus was always larger than that, one of community welfare, hence the African proverb "It takes a village."

The film also explores what researchers further determined; that greed once was considered a form of mental illness by ancient tribes and cultures, and secondly, that with the creation of greater wealth, we can become seduced by the notion that "more stuff" should equate to "more happiness." This idea has created what we see today—a world where greed is at the root of aggression, and unhappiness is far more prevalent in developed and prosperous nations. "Stuff" is clearly not what makes us happy and fulfilled; on the contrary, it is what we give, not what we have or receive which fulfills this DNA-commanded need. We intuitively know that contributing justifies our existence.

Without a sense of contribution we are off-kilter, dissatisfied and feel less than fully alive. In many studies evaluating happiness, acts of contribution and service to others are large predictors of overall happiness and capable of staving off depression. Giving *is* receiving, as the saying goes, because the act of giving fills us with numerous emotions: love, pride, satisfaction, hope, a sense of purpose to name a few. These emotions are all genetically engineered chemical responses in our brain that occur as a result of these acts. Serotonin, dopamine, GABA and oxytocin are but a few of the chemicals released that create a positive experience and response in our brains. Our contributions also create our legacies, where we leave our personalized mark in the world. Again, chemical mediators are released when we achieve what we aspire to. Being under the influence of such mediators is transformative, it's nature's own cluster of "feel good" drugs.

The transformative effect of contribution can be cultivated in homes, in workplaces and in relationships. The best way to inspire contribution from others is to be an example of the endless large and small ways contributions can be executed. "Be the change you wish to see," said Gandhi. Furthermore, when we acknowledge acts of contribution made by others and how it positively impacted us, we can motivate others to repeat more of the same.

Contribution is not just the act itself. Motivation and temperament are equally important. Many of us contribute in similar ways, but not everyone experiences satisfaction in doing so. We may in fact become resentful about it if our reasons for contributing are unmet. Sometimes, our lack of satisfaction may exist simply because we fail to recognize the importance of our contributions, or, we do not let it count until others recognize us for it. I believe these are often some underlying reasons we experience burnout. Leaders especially, those who are always facing forward in efforts to achieve more, may miss the results of having dropped a pebble of contribution in their pond. They simply aren't looking back to notice when the ripples finally hit the shore.

If we really want to cultivate personal excellence and obtain the satisfaction it can bring, we must grow our own internal sense of appreciation for our contributions, one that functions *independently* of external validation. There has to be a spirit of generosity and willingness to reap those internally generated rewards. Once we learn this, we no longer need the recognition of others. We keep the scorecard, we know our contributions, we give because we want to and because we know it feels good. We do not need to talk about it to feel the win. It simply bears witness to our acts, enabling us to pause and enjoy the delight of having contributed. Another very interesting thing also shown in this research is that when we pause and relive these moments, "feel good" chemical mediators are released once again in our brains giving us a renewed sense of happiness.

As science discovers the subtleties of energy, we are learning even our very thoughts are things that contribute to our environments. A fascinating study on water crystal formation comes from Japan where Dr. Masaru Emoto documented research in his book, *Messages Of Water*. His experiments exposed pure water to various words, prayers and music while being frozen. Crystals formed in bright, beautiful and symmetrical patterns with positive words, prayers and classical music. Conversely, they formed disorganized and brown in color with negative words, statements of hate and forms of discordant music. More astounding is that he was able to replicate these results just thinking these thoughts up to twenty five feet away. The research infers that how we are thinking and what we are saying translates to the world around us, contributing to and creating the reality experienced. There are also many psychology research conclusions which show how choosing to change a negative attitude to positive, impacts on the environment around us, influencing it to be more positive, ultimately making us feel more productive and energized. We, like the water crystals, become organized, bright and beautiful—a direct reflection of what we are giving. If we don't like what we are getting, we have to look at what we are giving to change our experience.

We are a sum total of our contributions. They need not be grand, tangible or highly visible. Contribution can be as random and small as the piece of trash we pick up so it can be disposed of properly. It may be a small word of encouragement, offering a smile or opening a door for someone. These are acts of significance since these little things of how we are in the world tally up and promote our own well-being, as well as the well-being of the world around us. Every second of every day we influence our environment through our thoughts and acts of contribution. Being conscious and deliberate to assure these thoughts and acts are positive and constructive IS the task. Find your niche, your own brand of contribution, know without doubt that what you do matters and savor where you see it having impact, even if you go unrecognized by others for it. Achieving the deepest sense of happiness depends on your ability to do so.

••• 6 •••

The "Law Of Attraction" And Beginning With The End In Mind

"Life can be pulled by goals just as surely as it can be pushed by drives."

Viktor Frankl

SO WHAT MORE do you want to achieve in your life? Not really sure? Well, you're not alone. In fact, studies show that only 20% of Americans set goals for themselves. Is it any wonder then that we feel a bit dissatisfied in the context of having little clarity about where we are going and what we want to achieve? It's a bit like bumbling around in the dark. But when we focus on ideal outcomes, or "beginning with the end in mind," we naturally begin to see opportunities that we would have missed had we been unclear. There also seem to be mysterious serendipities at work when we clearly imagine...you know, how things just seem to fall in place, happenstance meetings with just the right person or things that come to us just at the right time.

Albert Einstein said, "Imagination is more important than facts." It was his ability to imagine what was thought of as factually impossible that became the fertile soil of his genius. It was in that gap between known fact and imagined reality that he began to see possibility and relationship between known and unknown. His theories and the scientific experiments that followed radically altered our views of matter, light, gravity and energy. This evolved into what is known as quantum mechanics—the not so well understood subatomic nature comprising the universe. It also gave rise to a concept called the Law of Attraction, based on the quantum theory observation that like energy attracts like energy. Some may believe that the Law of Attraction is some sort of hocus-pocus belonging to New Age thinkers. What cannot be denied are the scientifically validated quantum mechanics effects. We have to be open and wise enough to know that absence of proof is not proof of absolute absence. Just because we haven't proven it so, does not prove it false. There simply is not enough data at this point, but it is gaining in credibility the more we understand the forces at play. These theories illustrated in the movies *What the Bleep Do We Know* and *The Secret* are presented in easily understood ways. Though I too would like to see more proof of the concepts, I found their content compelling and thought provoking. The theory is that when we create the thought energy of a specific goal, the compatible energies surrounding us respond and provide because they are attracted to it. I have empirically tested the theory and I have to say, whether scientific or psychological, it's effective for creating the life I want. Because this has been my experience, I would like to discuss it here and how to apply these theories in your own life to test out. The benefits are far reaching and worth the effort.

Endpoint clarity is critical to begin the process and engage the Law of Attraction. Any advance in the current world has always begun with an idea in the mind of a single person. It was viewed as pure whimsy when in 1480 Leonardo da Vinci drew the first rendition of what we now call a helicopter. Its ultimate creation came in 1907 when Paul Cornu created it as a consequence of his clarity of the end result—a flying machine enabled to go up, down and hover, as well as forward, right and left. Leonardo was genius enough to think that placing a rotor blade on top likely held the possibility, similar to 400 B.C. Chinese toys. It took centuries to figure it all out, but those who did were flexible enough in their thinking to keep trying different applications until success was achieved. Their focus remained steadfast that it *was* indeed possible...and they were dogged enough to keep gnawing on the problem until it was solved.

Whether the goal is a simple task or a big project, the practice of visualizing the end result and having flexibility in how we get there is the basis of successful problem resolution. It is important to place our focus on what we want, rather than what we don't want, because remember, like attracts like. If we focus on the current state, wallowing in the problem itself, dissecting it and trying to fix a problem from there, we will more often just design another set of problems and become vulnerable to the many rabbit holes that can either temporarily or permanently derail us from the sought-after objective. It is in consistently envisioning the desired *end result* as we work toward a goal that allows the "how to" of a plan to develop creatively, sometimes with out-of-the-box ideas. That frame of mind can even attract serendipitous circumstances that all collude to create what we imagined. The mind becomes much freer to conjure up ideas when it views things from the desired endpoint. We can also more clearly see the barriers keeping us from that endpoint. Creativity thrives and alternate avenues to get there arise.

My own observation of the Law of Attraction began when I started to evaluate my role in creating both positive and negative life experience relative to how I thought about things. It started with hearing the quote, "If you don't like what you are getting, look at what you are giving." I began to notice the many ways in which like attracts like seemed to play out in my own life. Focusing on what I didn't like or want brought more of the same. In that state I remained frustrated that "things never change."

When I started to imagine with greater clarity how I wanted things to be and began earnestly rejecting negative thoughts, I made progress. In fact, I got where I wanted to go much faster and with much more serendipity—kind of like taking a random exit ramp and voila'...a Starbucks, just when I was hankering for a cup of coffee. It was even sometimes humorous how things "just worked out" in my life. Over and over it was demonstrated to me that this simple truth is how life seemed to work. The principle can be applied to anything; be it a versatile flying machine, a more effective working relationship with someone, a better system to manage a process, greater prosperity, or an improved performance in our work. I even began to approach the smallest of things, like "where is that sock?" with a clear picture of the end result in mind, like holding the missing sock in my hand. I soon found that lost socks were not as frequent as the stuff of laundry legends!

Physicians who are pioneers in surgery, whether they know it or not, practice this and may explain it this way: it begins with an "intuitive knowing" or suspicion of what is possible. By being so focused on the desired outcome and so intimately familiar with the subject, the route to achieving rises to the surface and in to view. Many such pioneers will also tell you of happenstance conversations or situations that "just so happened" during their problem solving time, which further clarified the success route. These surgical pioneers may never have tried the procedure before, but they make brilliant discoveries by trusting that knowing, and trying anyway, in spite of their fears or critics. There is some sort of faith at the root of it. That faith trusts that answers will come to make what is envisioned, real.

In my work as a nurse, having the crystal-clear goal of providing the best possible care is immensely helpful as well. Notice I did not say "saving lives" or "making a difference." Those endpoints are too narrow, for not every life will be saved nor will my efforts always make a difference in the ultimate outcome. With those goals I am likely to become overwhelmed when things don't go well or the unexpected arises. It is far better to focus on preparing to be the best and then offering my best, than to hold so tightly to how it all turns out. This approach helps me stay calm because I know I have prepared, and helps me remain resourceful and grounded in my abilities. I am better able to prioritize, problem solve and be flexible in my approach, which can result in surprising solutions to problems.

The end in mind concept also is true as we navigate the territories of relationships, whether personal or professional. In a difficult relationship I am facing, I ask, "What is the end result I desire with this person? Are my thoughts and actions working for or against that result? Am I giving what I want to receive?" It comes down to this: we must behave (thoughts/words/action) according to and in alignment with what we envision as the end result if we want to manifest it. Keeping important objectives in the forefront, like "I want to have an effective working relationship" with someone, is powerful as we navigate conflict. It is what keeps us from thoughtlessly reacting to the smaller bits of a problem, such as when something doesn't go as expected or how something was said. When we keep the end result in mind, our actions and choices will more likely line up at the right time, in the right way. We will respond to the important stuff and let the trivial go. If we are more driven by wanting to "win", "be right" or make sure others know we are "top dog," we create blind spots that have us ending up with a different end result that doesn't ultimately better things or satisfy. We instead create alienation, squelch the desire for positive contribution in others or create subordinates that stop working *with* us and begin working—begrudgingly— *for* us or even against us.

Every day, usually with my first cup of coffee, I spend three to ten minutes visualizing what I want in my life. Focusing on the big and bold goals, I go through all of it – my career, my marriage, my health, my prosperity, my spirituality—and I imagine them in what I consider their ideal state with all the specific elements and emotions that I want with them. I also practice this in a smaller way when I have an important task to do, like a crucial conversation, or when I am on my way to work and want to change a habit or practice. I visualize the kind of nurse and coworker I want to be, again with all the positive emotion and feelings I will have *being* that kind of nurse or coworker. Doing so allows me to be clear and committed to the end result and motivates me because *I want* to feel that way, *I want* to have that positive experience. Having clarified the end results helps me stay on track later in my day when I ask myself, "Is what I am doing now getting me closer to what I really want?"

Understanding that we truly are the creators of our experience means we understand how the focus of our thoughts drives the experience. *Everything* in our lives first begins with thought, be it positive or negative, and those thoughts then begin to shape our reality. When we make it a habit to construct our thoughts consciously and positively with our goals and dreams in mind, our ability to create a life we love is unstoppable. One of my great mentors for this practice is Mike Dooley, whose tag line is "Thoughts become things, choose the good ones!" And it was wise Jane Goodall who said, "You cannot get through a single day without having an impact on the world around you. What you do makes a difference, and you have to decide what kind of difference you want to make."

This chapter is only the tip of the iceberg and it is not a weekend project to make it manifest in our lives. It, like anything worthwhile, takes practice, effort and external support to remind us of it and stay on track. I believe that the Law Of Attraction is at the top of the list of things to master if you want to create a life you love and fully enjoy. You can find additional resources to develop this practice on my website www.cjsnow.net

The Role of Idealism When Creating

It was Bono who said, "You see, idealism detached from action is just a dream. But idealism allied with pragmatism, with rolling up your sleeves and making the world bend a bit, is very exciting. It's very real. It's very strong." This is the kind of end in mind mentality we have been discussing.

Cynicism can make us resigned to "that's just the way things are." We may hold the notion that striving for ideal states may appear to be a form of arrogance, Pollyannaish or will leave others behind, making them feel inferior. All these views are targeting, and settling for, mediocrity. We try to comfort ourselves by explaining to ourselves that there is no hope for anything better (the cynic,) that we should expect the worst (the pessimist,) or that we shouldn't be overly ambitious so that everyone "feels good" about whatever lackluster contribution they make (the placator.) I would counter that the opposite is true. It is because of our settling for less that we are irritable, ill at ease, feeling hopeless and are haunted by a feeling that we are somehow declining and that our lives lack purpose and legacy.

Regardless of our level of personal awareness, the innate need to strive for something better gnaws at the soul of who we are. If we as a society abandon the pursuit of ideals and excellence, we will begin to slowly rot and die from the inside out. Setting the bar high and consistently striving for better, no matter what your personal "better" is, is the manna our spirits seek and will fuel us in ways unimaginable. If we are not looking for ways to raise the bar in the moment-by-moment opportunities of our lives, that bar will insidiously slip lower and lower, sometimes without our even noticing. It is through the pursuit of excellence that we gain momentum, just the acts involved in striving for an idealized life can leave us feeling energized and satisfied. I believe this is because of an innate need to evolve, and our efforts to offer our best creates momentum. Like a flywheel, getting it turning may be the hard part, but once in motion it requires less energy to be sustained in motion.

Life is not about being perfect, so there is no need to be discouraged when things don't turn out exactly as we imagined them. Life is about having done better than the last time we tried, moving closer to the perfection we imagine or doing something consistently well. History shows us that dreamers made the world we know today. Our ideal vision may not fully materialize in the short run, but designing a life around what we idealize most, working to get as close as possible to that vision, is a life evolving.

A Person Improved

I've heard it said that the only person you should try to be better than is the person you were yesterday. It's no small job committing to self-improvement and the pursuit of ideal states. It takes courage, self-discipline and accepting our imperfections with grace. It means we are dedicated to living as life-long learners, continual investors in the capital of Self and fearless appraisers of our progress. It is a waste of life's opportunities to accept mediocrity as sufficient. It seems to me a cheating of the human spirit.

For many though, there is no thought about rising to whatever potential they have; they just plod along, meeting the absolute minimum, simply "getting by." There are no dreams or aspirations—plenty of wishes perhaps, like winning the lottery—but the effort exerted in life is just enough so a paycheck comes in, trudging along in a dull and automated life. This seems so sad! Everyone has the right to choose the life they want of course, but I have to wonder...is that really the life they want?

If we desire a life full of vibrant color and legacy, one where we feel we have achieved something special, it's a matter of seeking out the limits of our potential. We can compel ourselves to go farther and farther until we find that place where we seem to fail, and then push ourselves some more. Our value of self is enhanced and our belief in the potential of others will also increase. It is a wonderful thing to discover that you're capable of something you had doubts about. So get to class, read your journals, go to conferences, certify, do some personal development work, work on your relationship problems, challenge yourself...all of it will spark enthusiasm for more when approached positively with the end in mind. Exceptionalism blossoms here, legacies are created and life gets really juicy.

In my own life, the landmark transition to embrace ideal-ism and pursue excellence happened like this: At the time, I was excelling in my professional life and achieving many of my sought-after achievements, I had found my wonderful husband, the right house, etc. Though many of my sought-after dreams were being realized, I had this gnawing sense of lack. I couldn't really figure out what was missing. I had an opportunity to hear a guest speaker at my church, who happened to operate a per-sonal development company that offered seminars as an avenue for personal growth. The concepts of ownership, being fully present, creating more of what I wanted in my life did not fully make sense at the time, but it piqued my interest so I put my money down and signed up for my first four-day seminar.

It was, and I am not exaggerating here, the absolute BEST gift I have ever given myself. Yeah, it was a bit scary to dissect how I was living my life, but I got over it. I began to pursue improving myself as a person in a very conscious way, learning many of the principles I am sharing with you. This started a journey of per-sonal betterment that continues to this day. I eventually went to several intensive four- and five-day seminars and eventually managed seminar logistics for the company, which kept me par-ticipating in the work. This "all in" act toward making a better me certainly took the training wheels off in the pursuit of my personal best.

Professionally I was growing, too. I had the good fortune to land a job with an outstanding employer where I would at last become a flight nurse aboard a 911 helicopter. The expected level of excellence in practice was set at an intimidatingly high bar. It pressed me to a level of performance that I had not thought possible and I have some extreme stories and great memories as a result. A cornerstone of the company philosophy was that it wasn't enough to just do our best, we had to prepare to be the best. We trained extensively, the idea being that practice doesn't make perfect, it makes better and better. Additionally, my patient care was dissected after every flight and pretty much any learning potential that existed was capitalized on. Talk about idealism!

At first it was difficult and overwhelming. Adapting to this level of honing my performance took a while to embrace because all I could hear in the beginning was how I was not doing things correctly. Well, like forged steel, the fire and hammer were creating an edge in my practice that I had previously never imagined. I learned to embrace the concept that missing the mark could be the basis of learning. I came to accept in a deeper way that no one is always right. My job was to seek my best, and to learn when I missed something, and not to flog that dead horse but keep the lesson and move on.

In this process I learned many things about excellence and how it contributed to my overall happiness. The achievement of it depends as much on the learning and growth as it does on our ultimate performance. Over the course of my tenure there I morphed into a learning sponge, wholeheartedly invested in my growth and the honing of my skills. Excellence was cultivated because I was mentored to strive for more, to offer my best, and I embraced the necessity of working to maintain it. It's also where I learned that the height of excellence is reached when shared. The perfect synergy and thrill of a finely-tuned team was a frequent experience as a flight nurse for this company, and one I will never forget. This is where I *fully* began to love the practice of nursing and experienced so many of the concepts addressed in this book.

This is not to say that I didn't experience difficulties or areas where I struggled, but the continual effort at improving was key to creating a life and career that was enormously satisfying and one that I can look back on with pride. When I left that rigorous job, it was hard to continue without that same level of esprit de corps and be in cultures that lacked that kind of drive. It did, however, press me to advocate for the same practice where ever I was. I believe my devotion to the principles adopted there will always be a cornerstone of who I am and serve as a rock-steady point of reference for me.

I know not all of our workplaces are ideal and some are downright awful. Several workplace cultures I've experienced lack drive to excel. I have also seen shifts in culture when some of us stayed focused on what we hoped for, exerted influence where we could and began seeing how those sparks we created began building into a fire. More and better followed and those cultures improved.

Excellence is catching. When we stick with it, resolutely focused on the desired outcome, it will follow. When we let our lives speak, are examples of the principles we value and work to improve our own flaws, people notice. Cultivating ideal states to become "a person improved" and embracing idealism are choices we can make. We each have the independent ability to decide how we shall be.

··· 7 ···

Being Fully Engaged And Present In The Moment Provides Maximum Opportunity

"Live each present moment completely, and the future will take care of itself."

Paramahansa Yogananda

IT IS A skill to stay fully engaged and present in whatever moment we are in. 'Be here now' is the phrase. It's easy when life is proceeding in ways that are pleasing or exciting to us, or the importance of the task is so great it commands our attention. If we learn to be more present in all of our life, we become more capable of noticing the unexpected treasures, stress relievers and opportunities life is constantly providing. This kind of mindfulness takes practice to learn, but in learning to apply it I have found life to be not only more easily managed and fulfilling, but I also find myself more capable of recognizing the right opportunities when they come along. Let's face it: being focused on the unchangeable past or yet-to-be-determined future are not the places of influence in life. The present is the only place we can have impact.

Those of us living active lives tend to be in the habit of anticipation; we're future-focused on what's next. The nature of anticipation can make us impatient for what we're expecting or where we're going. We become occupied with worry about things turning out right. Both promote anxiety and distraction from the here and now.

Current studies from mental healthcare agencies estimate around 30% of the North American population between the ages of eighteen and fifty-five experience anxiety over the "what's next" on a regular basis. We all know that the future is not a sure thing, there are too many life-variables that can change things in a minute. C. T. Boom said it well: "Worry does not empty tomorrow of its sorrow. It empties today of its strength." The work is to pay attention to the moment and influence outcomes where we can.

Others of us are more focused on the past where memories can be a rabbit hole that we disappear into leading to regret and depression. The CDC estimates that one in ten Americans feel they are depressed and those numbers are increasing every year. Depression has also been determined to have a strong link with anxiety where nearly half of those experiencing depression also have anxiety issues. The WHO lists depression as the second leading cause of death in ages fifteen to twenty-nine. Excessive rumination around regret, shame and guilt are all past-fixated mindsets and hallmarks of depression. The next step is to grasp that the past cannot be changed. The work then is to accept it, forgive yourself or others for the transgressions, and learn what we can from those experiences.

Things like stage of life, cultural influence, economics, education, marital status and family history all seem to play a part in putting us at risk for anxiety and depression, but researchers admit these factors only tell part of the story. Those of us coming at the issue from a more holistic point of view hold the belief that our physical health and mental habits play a primary role in our vulnerability. Things like "happy habits", a clean diet, meditation and mindfulness all have been shown to enhance our neurochemical well-being and therefore our moods and experience of life.

Naturally favoring either the habit of being past or future focused depends largely on our personality traits, cultural conditioning and life circumstances. For most of us it's a long-standing habit to do so, and like most habits, a bit challenging to uproot. Most of us have never learned to manage our past/present/future focus appropriately, and many of us have little or no awareness of when we are in each state. It costs us dearly to be so unaware and changing that is what we're going to discuss here.

Future-focused attention has some obvious benefits, like time management, organization and enjoying the anticipatory excitement of something we're looking forward to. We need to plan, and there's nothing wrong with looking forward to something, but too much attention has a price. Past-focused attention affords us time to reflect and learn, or provides us pleasure in the reliving of a memory. Both are important to incorporate. Reliving positive memories is considered a "happy habit," but if we linger too long in either regret or pleasure, we become less attentive to what's being offered in the moment. Opportunities get missed and our ability to do the little things to create the life we want becomes diminished. It's pretty simple: the only real point of opportunity and power to influence and fully enjoy things, is in the present moment.

Let's examine a few scenarios to illustrate this. If I want to practice more kindness, incorporate a new nursing habit such as better informing my patients, or decide I want to make a point of recognizing others for their good works, all these require close attention to the current moment so I can notice places where I can deploy those things. If I want to spend meaningful time with others, I do so by putting aside past and future concerns and just enjoy them and the moment we have...even if it is only for a few minutes. If I am occupied with how efforts have failed in the past or am worried about failing again if I try, more than likely I'll completely miss the moments that afford me opportunity to accomplish exactly what I want.

Being fully engaged and present is not easy in our overly stimulating world. We should be cognizant of the many ways to mentally "check-out" with distractions that are meaningless, particularly when we invest significant time in them. Things like always having the TV on, obsessive texting, Facebooking ad nauseam, gaming and other forms of entertainment are all examples that can over-run our lives with distraction. While there is nothing wrong with some down time in distraction, we'd be smart to stay vigilant as to what we are neglecting in the process. If we find ourselves sitting on a park bench on a beautiful day absorbed in our phones, I would have you ask what feeds your humanness more, the phone or getting all wrapped up in the nature surrounding you?

I think we often lose sight of the simple things that can give us joy. Watching your child play, your dogs roughhouse, to see-feel-smell the elements of nature around you, these are all things that will satisfy you in a deeper and more meaningful way than the aforementioned activities if you take the time to *just be* in the moment. We are more likely to relax at a deeper level and feel more renewed when we do. On a physiologic level, these simpler activities have been shown to reset and calm down our stress hormones and promote the release of our own "feel good" chemicals.

Failing to live in the present moment has other implications. Think about how often we respond based on other concerns gnawing at us that have no direct relation to current events. I'm not sure there is a number high enough to quantify how many misunderstandings and life changing events that have occurred as a result of misplaced anger and angst.

Here are some important questions we should ask ourselves to get honest about our living-in-the-moment habits: Have I ever failed to recognize a kindness bestowed on me because I was "having a bad day"? How many times have I been so absorbed in the fear of things going wrong (future focused), or have been fearful because I have failed before (past focused), that I've been blind to the obvious or too frozen in fear to act? Are these past/future thoughts becoming so consuming that I have no more room in my head and heart to put forth a best effort in the moment? Am I habitually focused on what I am doing, or is my attention elsewhere? Having focus anywhere but in the present robs us of the chance to be optimally responsive to whatever is before us. It is much more natural for the right action to become apparent as the obvious next step when we are fully invested in current experience. Failure to see opportunity and to act is more likely when we lose sight of, lack commitment to, or are not clear about this principle of being present.

The greater our ability to live in the present, bringing with us all we have learned, the more apt we become at seizing opportunity. Couple that with a clear set of core values that you act in accordance with and you've just managed to employ the primary foundational elements to excel and find your perpetual sweet-spot. It not always easy to do, but preparing ourselves in this way fosters the ability to be brave when necessary or restrained when needed.

In a world where angst and worry are common feelings, I have found that my life has a lot less of them when I practice being fully present with whatever I'm engaged in. This is partly because I know I have placed myself in the best place to respond to whatever life brings my way so I feel, in a way, prepared. I also have greater ability to notice and enjoy the mini stress-reducers I encounter in an ordinary day, like friendship and things of beauty. When I remember that feeling anxious or down about things are signs of being focused on a yet-to-be-determined future or done-and-over past events, I can then see them for what they are—distractors that place me in a disadvantaged position. This empowers me to put them aside and focus on the here and now rather than letting those feelings overwhelm me.

Clarity more easily returns, I more adeptly act in accordance with what I value most and I read circumstances more accurately. This has me making fewer missteps, fewer "knee-jerk" or thoughtless responses and a clarity of mind that feels freer or less encumbered to conduct life. I spend far less time worrying about the future because confidence grows in my ability to choose wisely, because I do choose wisely more often. Living presently and aligned with my values helps me to more readily correct my course when off track because I see it sooner and am more aware of its importance. We even enhance our ability to learn in life when we bravely embrace the present in the face of missteps.

Living this way also helps us to process difficult events more easily, release them and move on. Forgiveness, of myself and others, comes more easily. Peace of mind comes with that.

There are entire books written about how to be fully present and I strongly encourage you to explore them[*]. If you find this kind of focus difficult to achieve, try meditation to help calm your mind and remove the fog of an over-stimulated life. If you have yet to explore the full depth of living presently, what awaits you is an untapped richness and position of power to make your life what you want. Those of you who are practitioners of it, join my blog and share with others what it has taught you.

Lastly, I would be remiss if I didn't emphasize how being fully present applies to enjoying times of relaxation as well and the sense of renewal we gain from it. The most precious parts of life become so much richer when we are fully present in them. Our world becomes bigger and our ability to take in all the beauty around us is enhanced when we pause without distraction to appreciate it. We see that there is so much more to our lives than just petty annoyances and this gives us a more balanced perspective. Try taking a moment to fully appreciate the innocence of your children or their profound youthful beauty. Try walking through a beautiful park, taking in the warmth of the sunshine,

---

[*]   Some book suggestions are listed on cjsnow.net

the majestic trees or the smell of rain. Observe your favorite pet enjoying a toy, how they relish lying in the sunshine or playing at the dog park. Take the time to listen to a dear friend with your whole heart and all of your attention. Living life this way creates more vivid memories that we are able to later revisit and gain pleasure from. Giving ourselves breaks like these expands our hearts, generates happiness, gives us balance, peace and perspective. So how 'bout it...you in?

PRACTICAL MATTERS:
"WHERE THE RUBBER MEETS THE ROAD"

NOTE TO MY READERS

Much of the content in this section exists because of what I have observed in the multiple heathcare venues I've worked in over the last forty years. We will explore causes of work culture issues and helpful strategies to cultivate a better one and how to course correct when needed. In my experience, most organizations do not do enough to cultivate a healthy work environment with cohesive, high-functioning teams. Work cultures are living things and require tending to on a day-to-day basis to keep healthy. I've observed the lack of tools to do this both in management and the frontline worker, and all too often have seen unhealthy uses of power in all directions; top down, laterally and from the bottom up. In earlier years, I had little idea about how to improve this or effectively deal with what I encountered. Given the duress it caused me and others, I was driven to learn more about what makes a great place to work where everyone strives to offer their best. Some of you may view what is covered as "basic" good workplace practices. If you know these principles, I applaud you. You are ahead of the game. *Knowing* and actually *doing* are not synonymous however. Given what I've seen and continue to see, I'm compelled to discuss principles that are helpful so we can all foster healthier environments in a conscious way. We can do better. We should do better. Caregivers need and deserve environments that are supportive and healthy, which inevitably translates to better care for our patients.

... 8 ...

Some Days Are Just Difficult

"A person of character finds a special attractiveness in difficulty since it is only by coming to grips with difficulty that we can realize our potentials."

General Charles de Gaulle

IN SPITE OF our best efforts, there are certainly those days when nothing seems to go right. We may feel stressed, perpetually behind, or feel that we have failed to offer our best. In nursing, I take it personally when the care offered was lacking, usually because there were just not enough resources to support the process. While there is often enough blame to pass around, to focus on that in the moment is usually not helpful. Sometimes we have to humbly surrender and accept that "it is what it is" and let it go if we are to survive our current circumstances with grace.

Such circumstances are certainly rising in their frequency and I would hope that we all have a proportionate crescendo in our alarm over the situations we face in today's healthcare. Many practitioners have left their fields because of it. It truly is a call to action as patriots of quality care delivery. We will be most happy with ourselves and our circumstances if we contribute to solutions. Speak up with ideas to remove the barriers through committee actions and advocacy. Get involved in making it better. At very least work on yourself so you are not enabling the dysfunction. I relate to the quote above. I would never want an opportunity to pass me by without capitalizing on it, so I have learned to turn these difficult days into character building experiences and places where I hone my nursing practice and my personal resilience. The challenges I have felt on those sorts of days teach me things. It has also been what has propelled me to be part of the solution to cure what ails us.

Navigating some days seems impossible. We idealistically believe, as we should, that everyone should receive the same level of care. I don't know about your place of work but in the hospitals I've worked in, staffing shortages, flu epidemics and the overall rising numbers of patients to be seen often impacts us and to varying degrees overwhelms the system. It is a sad reality that not every patient will receive optimal care. The point is to offer the best possible care given our set of circumstances.

It can be a blurry line between excuses and elements that truly are beyond our control. Consistently offering our best means we take ownership of what we can control and give things our best effort to do right, even though we may be lacking in resources, are tired, progress is thwarted or are otherwise deficient in gusto. Excellence may be our target, but sometimes the distance we find ourselves aiming from is simply too far away to hit the bull's eye. What matters in being a caregiver with integrity, is to focus on what we can do to improve matters. Just as General de Gaulle said, we can "realize our potentials" in those difficulties. Just as in forging metal where it becomes stronger with repeated application of fire and hammer, we too can become stronger and more resilient through these experiences.

I am not suggesting that difficult days should be your everyday reality or that self-critiquing is a beat-yourself-up session. We do, however, benefit from a dispassionate dissection of our performance either in the moment or in our review of the day. No hitter in a baseball season ever bats 1,000, and neither do nurses, doctors, mechanics or our partners. Accepting the impossibility of true perfection does take a level of maturity and perspective.

A habit of self-review is one that I deploy daily in life in and out of work. It is especially helpful when it comes to critical events and life challenges. If I see flaws in how things turned out, I start an evaluation process: Where did I start to get off track? Where could I have been preemptive? What changes need to be made in my habit patterns? It *was* a horrible day, but were there places to improve my planning, attitude and commitment? What can I bring up to managers, committees or my partner to enhance our performance and maximize resources? Where can I contribute to the solution? Incorporating some of these questions as we work through the day can be helpful to maintain a constructive mentality. It frames things toward the positive instead of fixating on the negative. When I conclude my self-review, I make a plan to influence the outcome differently next time. I may even journal about it because I find the learning sticks better when I do. What's most important about this kind of ownership and self-review is that when done with compassion and without blame, we are more capable of removing barriers that limit our success. We're human, we make mistakes, we have limitations. It's what we do next time that matters.

Tough experiences will recur. Life will never be all we idealize. Some situations can push us to the brink. Some of us become burnt out and discouraged over this, feeling as if we will never succeed. This kind of self-defeat is in part based on the faulty premise that excellence has been thought of as getting it right 100% of the time. We are truly delusional for thinking this way, it's simply not humanly possible. It is, admittedly, difficult to accept in types of work where the consequences involve human lives.

Happiness and satisfaction are sustainable if we become proficient at finding a place of peace with the hard parts of life. Learning to accept experiences will help us avoid a default position of cynicism. This is not resignation. It's a process of accepting life's imperfections, while also delving into honest evaluation for improving circumstances and integrating the fact that we are not perfect.

This is not a verbal massaging of the truth that gets us off the hook when we miss the mark. What I'm saying is, what is done is done. Learn from it, strategize for better and move on. There will often be things out of our control no matter how hard we try. Some days are just difficult. Failure is not in falling down, but in refusing to get up.

The Power Of Surrender And Allowing What Is

Sharon Stone, a well-known actress, had a debilitating stroke at age forty-three. When talking about her arduous recovery, she said this: *"You want to be a Champion? Let the things that are already here work for you."* Effectively deciding what to do and facilitating our own growth requires that we start with an accurate assessment of reality. Resisting "what is" can escalate frustration and keep us working *against*, rather than *with* what we face. To come to a place of possibility, we have to find a way to allow and embrace things as they are, no matter how screwed up we think they may be. Refusing to accept things as they stand is like trying to get directions without knowing your current location—absolutely useless.

"Surrendering" is not synonymous with giving up and I know at least a few of you bristle at that word. This is not the kind of surrender that means we lie down, give up or condone circumstances we cannot in good conscience overlook. It means to stop resisting things as they are, allow it to be what it is, and constructively work with circumstances to build on whatever solid ground we can find. It is a matter of adaptability, a key to our continued existence and ability to thrive. Adaptability means we are willing to look honestly at our circumstances and manage how we are *internally* responding to them. Adapting is a state of non-resistance. There's no obsessing over the rightness or the wrongness of something. To deny what is before us, or rail against it, only wastes energy, time and fuels frustration. "Work with what ya got," making it better, finding a way to influence change, has to begin with what *you do* have. One familiar example of this principle is found in the hugely successful, more than seventy-year-old Twelve Step program for addiction; Step One is all about identifying and owning that there is an addiction. Assessing and embracing that element is foundational for the rest.

"What you resist, persists." The more time we spend focused on what is wrong, resisting it through our judgments, assigning blame, being mad at and refusing to simply observe things as they really are, the longer it will stay just as it is. In some cases, it may even get worse because anger and judgement can fuel such fires. No movement toward something better occurs in this state. This is precisely how we stay stuck.

How many times in our workplaces do we create what we think is a solution, only to discover that we have created a whole new set of problems, or just a new layer of difficulty? It can be frustrating and quite a disappointment! The failure is often because we don't honestly embrace existing limitations or unsolved problems underlying our current difficulty. Problems have to be worked back to their origins with perspectives taken from every level of its creation. They also require the involvement of those on the receiving end of what we are trying to fix. Unfortunately, those impervious to the results of decisions often believe they are the best equipped to make them, not realizing that their imperviousness comes with blind spots.

While it may on the surface seem like the long way around to approach problems this way, I can assure you it will be in the avoidance of new problems that you will find efficiency. It's when we are willing to look at all the realities as they are, that we find a more effective way to take them on. Possibility more easily arises and the problem's resolution begins to take shape organically when we understand how we got there in the first place.

As I practice these concepts in my own life, I notice an ever-increasing ability to adapt to and overcome problems. Whether I am faced with a challenging relationship problem or a patient's emergency, I am increasingly better able to stay calm and come up with the correct action. Learning to surrender, or to "be in allowance of" people and circumstances as they present themselves, helps me be more capable of staying on an even keel. I can more clearly focus on and work toward the desired outcome.

Approaching things in this way can also help us to enter what many top performers refer to as "the zone" or what psychologists call "flow state." Flow is a state of being so fully present that we forget about judgments, worries and fears that often create our perceived limitations. This laser focus on the present enables us to see possibilities others may not because our resourcefulness is optimized. This approach also effectively manages our emotions and worries about getting it wrong or if we will be successful. They stay in the background where their influence is mitigated. This is where we tap into our own ingenious and creative selves. This is the exquisite art of surrendering and being in allowance of all that is. Here is where we can effectively move forward.

Understanding Our Circle Of Influence

Part of surviving hellish days, overcoming problems with grace and finding that place of acceptance and peace comes from understanding our circle of influence. It begins with accepting that about the only thing we have full control over is what we ourselves think, say and do. It's true that we have to let go of things truly beyond our control. That being said, letting go does not mean we forego our abilities to influence. Letting go without considering any action to influence a situation may even function as an excuse for not exerting the effort required to influence things where we can. Letting go in this way and not advocating for better, can evolve to feelings of inadequacy, resignation, cynicism, even clinical depression. I believe this is the cause for many of us to lose heart and is at the core of burnout affecting healthcare providers across the country. Letting go in this way leaves us stuck, devoid of possibility and hope.

The sense of hopelessness to change for the better pervades many of our workplaces today. In healthcare we often believe there are too many factors against us, the problem too massive to address or "above our pay grade" to solve. We can become so completely focused on the problems, obsessed with what is wrong that we lose sight of what can be done to create a better experience. This perspective sadly evolves, to a "woe-is-me" victim mentality in many institutions, where we buy into the idea that we are helpless to create a different experience. We forget that our perspectives and attitudes can change our personal experiences dramatically, and in turn affect the conditions around us. Creating real change happens with one small effort at a time—it starts within us and in our internal environment which translates into our perspectives and actions. Even making small, daily practices to support our internal serenity can be powerful, thereby creating a basis to shift the culture of a workplace. Such efforts are within our circle of influence.

When we fail to act or work toward what we believe in, or fail to do something courageous that promotes an ideal, we may unconsciously despise that failing. We loath our inaction, lack of courage and can even feel a subtle shame in our failure to seek out what *is* in our control. It is a position of apathy, which can in turn become despair. We may settle for apathy and despair because it is too uncomfortable to honestly look at where we failed to act and influence where we could. Living life in a way where our actions of contribution are visible, is living in full ownership of the very real fact that we have a great degree of influence in how our life is experienced.

It also helps to have a work environment where folks are supported to create better. Wise leadership recognizes this and supports employees to lead on projects and express their passion for improvements from their point of reference. Individual contribution is to be encouraged, even celebrated by the group. Squelching it is a mistake. People usually rise further in their potentials when we trust and inspire them to do so.

On the flip side, thinking we have to take ownership of things that are out of our control can result in us feeling overwhelmed and produce an anxiety that has countless people on anti-anxiety and anti-depressant medications. Events and their associated drama consume us and we moan and carry on about how awful it is. Social media and news sources can fan these flames, leaving many of us wallowing in the constant complaint of what is wrong and dramatizing every nuance.

If we become preoccupied with things out of our control, it can create a paralyzing inertia, or conversely, an anger and agitation which may become violent. Both foster a culture of blame, division and disharmony. In this state we fail to consider what our seemingly small, individual actions can do to alter the outcome simply because we are looking for solutions beyond our actual reach. Trends to violently destroy things in protest, violate the rights of individuals because we don't agree with them and the advocation for incivility coming from so-called leaders is hugely concerning and an end-product of victim perspectives. If we want change, we have to start with "being the change," offering the kind of treatment we ourselves want to those around us. Violence begets violence—period. Most of our attention should be on the kind of wake *our* actions leave behind, because that's how an individual can make a difference.

At an organizational level, leaders will best serve the world and their organizations by approaching culture correction from this "inside-out" perspective. We can mandate all the correct behaviors we want of civility and service, but those behaviors cannot take root if employees are not motivated from within to adopt them. The work lies in convincing them why these are valuable. Generating that kind of motivation comes from supporting the most basic need of all people: to feel loved and respected. (Often leadership overlooks or feels uncomfortable with the idea of "love" belonging in the workplace. But the kind of love I am talking about is based in compassion, treating others as we would like to be treated.) Even when administering corrective action this should be our guiding principle. Concepts of kindness, being helpful, tolerance of and appreciation for differing personality styles, forgiveness and wanting to understand each other can more naturally arise when individuals are supported to have balanced lives and are consistently shown love and respect. Too often in organizations our focus is on "fitting in," rather than valuing individuality. We are weakened when we want sameness and are intolerant of differing perspectives and styles.

Our world consists of ever-changing variables. Simply by being physically present we exert influence, as it was shown with Emoto's freezing water. Even so, we can only hope to control or influence a certain number of variables. In medicine, every patient is different and bodies respond to care in their unique way. It benefits us to embrace the fact that not every patient will respond positively to our help. This is just as true in all relationships. The stakes may not be as high, but we all have limits to our influence and control in any given situation. Stay focused on offering *your* best and ask yourself "what can *I* do?" Focusing on what we can do puts us in a more powerful position and helps us recognize where we can influence for the better in the given moment. It gives us the satisfaction that we have done our best. This habit will effect positive changes and outcomes, one contact or challenge at a time.

Celebrate Your Victories On The Homefront

While all this honest evaluation for improvement is indispensable to achieving our personal best, it is equally important to enjoy and celebrate the wins. Reflecting on what we did well and reflecting on where we made a positive difference is vital. Permit that satisfied smile to linger a bit on your face as you reflect on things done well. Celebrating successes and noticing where we made things better balances our psyche, aids in releasing some of those feel-good neurochemicals and gives us the affirmation that we are capable of positive influence in this demanding world. Let in the good feelings of having done things well, no matter how small. It will nurture your spirit. No one ever said that being humble means we have to forgo the appreciation of having done something well. Some days may have less than others to recount, but no matter how few the victories, it is important to celebrate and savor each as they give us the confidence to go back and give effort to tomorrow. As silly as it may sound, on my really exceptional days I tell my dogs all about it when I get home. I clap my hands and dance around while they bark and carry on—that's how we celebrate circle of influence in the Snow household!

After evaluating my day, planning for better and celebrating the good, I let it all go and release what the day has brought. It makes it exponentially easier to live and fight another day when I can shelve it as a day of learning *and* some successes—however small they may be. Being able to release what is done and over, opens the door for our much deserved and necessary rest, relaxation and rejuvenation. This grounded approach gives rise to the satisfaction of a life well lived and generates the enthusiasm to keep growing, exerting our best effort to influence where we can.

When we are clear about our abilities and focus on what we can control we become more measured in how we do business and our circle of influence is likely to expand. People notice the clarity of intention, the deliberateness of action and the eloquence of responsiveness we exhibit when we are grounded in this way. Reactivity is noticeably less or absent when we become this intentional. It is then easier for people to hear us and our influence grows.

Perhaps the nicest part of understanding our circle of influence is that we fret less about the stuff beyond our control. When we focus and apply ourselves to making a difference where we can, we become more willing to accept where we can't. We become freer to experience the richness of our lives because we pay attention to the stuff that matters most.

The Giant Influential Spheres Of Fame, Position And Parenting

Seemingly overnight our sphere of influence can expand when we assume roles in management, become famous, get elected, enter a profession or become parents. It is unfortunate when those with this sort of influence lack integrity, live their lives unconsciously, speak when ill-informed or have no clue as to what their core values are, let alone live by them. Such carelessness and lack of integrity is precisely what can drive the need for distraction and drugs leaving many despairing and unhappy. So, if we assume such roles, it's even more critical that we do our own work to evolve as consciously living beings. Having that kind of power and ability to shape the world around us is a big responsibility and letting your life speak takes on even grander dimensions.

Influence is a living thing, always expanding or contracting in response to our thoughts, words, deeds, roles and circumstances. The clearer we become about what matters to us and the more we understand how we influence, the more our actions shape a positive experience. When we are faithful to our own betterment and our responsibility to the world we live in, we have greater peace under the weight of our responsibilities. This is the source of true power to heal and influence positive changes in ourselves and others. This is what affords us survival with grace during those difficult days.

... 9 ...

Navigating Conflict Without Blame And The Power Of Ownership

"People take different roads seeking fulfillment and happiness. Just because they're not on your road doesn't mean they've gotten lost."

The Dalai Lama

OFTEN WHEN WE are in the position of taking action to influence what we can, the worry of conflict arises. Speaking up or countering the opinion of another can create varying degrees of discomfort both for the giver and receiver. Part of this discomfort may be due to the concern that some believe a differing opinion is the enemy. Because of this many people avoid speaking up. We may accept the status quo rather than run the risk of conflict, being disenfranchised or enduring the discomfort a differing opinion can bring. Are we losing our capacity to have debate where the explored merits of a position can carry the day? When did we decide a differing opinion means we are in conflict?

Just because we choose to avoid conflict doesn't mean it goes away. Instead, the energy often morphs. It can become gossip, or degrade to subtle acts of passive-aggressive sabotage, moodiness, overt hostility and stress-related physical disorders. We might be like Woody Allen who said, "One of my problems is that I internalize everything. I can't express anger, I grow a tumor instead!" While what we may want to express might not necessarily be anger, our fear of confrontation or rejection and the neglect of issues often converts to counterproductive emotions or disease states. Dr. Neha Sangwan MD, in her book *Talk Rx* , explores the relationship between disease and our ability to communicate. She explains in her writing that without appropriate, honest and clear communication, unresolved issues persist and ultimately transmute into some form of "dis-ease" within our bodies, a "dis-eased" workplace or a "dis-eased" relationship. Again I ask, who decided that a differing viewpoint equates to conflict? This belief is an oppressive way of thinking because it either fosters our own insecurities to speak our truth because we do not want to create conflict or it implies that there is some sort of insistence that we are saying is right. And why is it in that moment that we often forget all the things that we *do* agree upon?

Any decent person wants to avoid upsetting another. Being kind and good has always been associated with peace and harmony, but are we really kind and good when our default position is to always agree or remain silent? This oversimplification has us thinking that harmony depends upon having a unified perspective and never having an opposing opinion. That's just not realistic if we truly believe that everyone should have a voice. It's good to have our opinions challenged because our evolution and progress would be horribly crippled without it. Is there anything in our natural world that is without opposing forces? It is a requirement of all creation to have them. These forces keep the balance of spinning atoms and perpetuate the continued existence of all things. It's their very synergy of polarization that creates everything.

Do ideas different from our own make us wrong or someone else wrong? As is often the case, we simply haven't learned how to talk to each other when differing opinions or difficulties arise. Learning to speak to issues in honest and respectful ways **and** having the ability to hear and consider opposing positions is where true cooperation lies. I've heard it said that fools argue, the wise discuss, and that is terrific advice. The ability to discuss is where we can sustain emotional balance, grow and thrive. As Dr. Sangwan suggests, we must "get comfy with discomfort" to effectively communicate. If we can be comfortable with changing our perceptions when a new perspective becomes clear, and brave enough to admit when we are wrong or had a lopsided view of things, then facing or being confronted with an opposing idea is not so big and scary. It's simply a discussion of viewpoint and consideration of things we may have not fully considered. If we can reframe or change how we view opposing ideas as a naturally occurring and necessary opposition of forces that keeps everything in balance, then we have an acceptable and natural way of existing and evolving, and our sense of personal threat decreases.

Tough Love, Enabling And Accountability

I remember watching an interview of Diane Sawyer. Something she said stuck with me: "A criticism is a really bad way of making a request, so why not just make the request?" I found it helpful advice.

There has been much education and discussion regarding the idea of tough love, enabling, and accountability. The same principles hold true in our professional lives as in our private lives. We enable bad behavior when we avoid dealing with it and fail to realize the disservice this imposes not only on the person misbehaving, but also the relationship, the organization, the people in the organization, and those the organization serves. Communicating in kind and respectful ways, requesting what it is we want, as Ms. Sawyer puts it, is an important piece of skillfully avoiding conflict when something needs to improve. Requesting rather than criticizing is more likely to move a person forward.

Accountability for our own actions and the willingness to ask others to do the same is not synonymous with oppression. Yet, we often balk at attempting honest communication because asking for accountability may be interpreted as condescension. That small mental shift of making a request naturally leans us towards kind and respectful communication.

I remember a coworker I once had, whom I'll call Sandra, who was known for a lax team spirit, rarely helping others and preferring to spend her periods between nursing tasks on the phone, talking or texting. There came a pivotal day when I watched her continue her personal pursuits while another nurse, whom I'll call Clara, and I shifted into high gear to get a heart attack victim transferred to the Cardiovascular Lab.

While we were focused on this emergency, Sandra did not check in to see if our other five patients needed anything. As our day continued, Clara and I remained very, very busy while Sandra remained siloed in her own world, often sitting at the desk or in relaxed conversations with coworkers about things like their latest vacations or Friday night escapades.

Meanwhile, supplies became depleted and I felt frustration when I needed things and had to restock in the middle of trying to care for people. It was infuriating to be on the verge of being overwhelmed and not be offered help or support of any kind. I blurted out "We could use some supplies here!" to no one in particular hoping she would hear the subtext of my blurt. (To be clear, that DID NOT qualify as effective communication!) Though she was less than six feet away, she didn't even look up from her texting. I felt awkward addressing the behavior because I am not the boss, and I felt uncomfortable complaining to my supervisors if I hadn't at least tried to address the situation. I also wanted to maintain an effective work relationship with her and was afraid of being honest about my frustration. Wow, did I feel stuck... and irritated! Perhaps you can relate to some of this?

It took a few days to let go of the irritation and sort through the experience so I could figure out a course of action. The old me would have allowed my anger to drive a heated confrontation or at least a simmering resentment and gossip about the experience, but the newer me didn't want to be that angry girl. Most important though was that I didn't want this level of dysfunction to continue because of the impact it had to everyone involved, especially the patients who got less than they deserved. I thought about Johann Goethe, who said "Treat a man as he is and he will remain as he is. Treat a man as he can and should be, and he will become as he can and should be." I wanted to have an effective relationship with my colleague, I knew we could agree on the concept of a high functioning team and I wanted to invite her to participate more in effective team practices. Taking Goethe's, Sawyer's and Dr. Sangwan's advice, I focused on what I wanted to request of her, on concepts we could agree upon, and effectively nudge her forward to a coworker more aware and willing to help when she can.

A few days later I found a private moment with her and said, "Sandra, wow, that day we had last week was a whopper for me." I asked a few questions about her perceptions of the day's difficulty, to which she responded that she thought it was an "ordinary crazy day." "Well," I continued, "it was an exceptionally tough one for Clara and me. I wanted to talk with you because I think some of the difficulty could have been eased with a more cohesive team, one where we are really working together and having each other's backs. I want to be honest. When I saw you texting or having personal chats with others over the course of the day, I felt disappointed that you had not checked in to see if we or our patients needed any help. It was particularly difficult during the emergent heart attack transfer, and there were supply issues that also needed attention. I went home feeling really frustrated. What I would really like is for us to work together in a way where we check in with each other and make an effort to keep things running smoothly, as a team, so that we aren't killing ourselves when things are crazy around here."

Sandra is not a person who displays much emotion, but she paused for a minute, taking in what I said. "Yeah, I guess I didn't notice" was her response, which was silly given the close proximity of that unit. I let that statement go because it was not my goal to make her wrong. My goal was for her to start stepping up. "All right," I said, "thanks for hearing me out. This was hard for me because I like you, I want us to have a good relationship and I certainly don't want to alienate you. Thanks again for considering."

After that discussion a shift slowly occurred. I began to notice Sandra making an effort to be aware of the unit's needs and began offering help more frequently. She even later stepped up to a lead role and proved to be a good one. My less-than-wiser self would have just blasted her with all my judgements about her deficiencies, "Really? You didn't notice the six people around the man's bed, the ambulance crew and the secretary's calls, who was sitting right next to you, to the Cath Lab? Really?" If I had let that fly the end result would likely have been animosity. But noticing the judgements I had about the situation gave me the ability to rise above the need for condemnation and approach her in a more productive way. Giving her an opportunity to rise above was kind, appropriate and produced a mutually beneficial result. Accountability existed for both Sandra and I. I was accountable because I made the effort to foster a team that is maximally effective, and she became more aware and accountable for her part in making an effective team who provides good patient care. And, creating that did not require a conflict to achieve it.

Everyone has a role in fostering a happier workplace and one where patients are safer. The same applies to our relationships. It takes a willingness to be diligent and patient as it can take a few days or months to accomplish—maybe even years—but is worth the effort. Not addressing issues effectively results in a slow slide backwards. People become resentful, patients are more at risk and our workplaces are not enjoyable. Teams that foster accountability through effective communication and who confront issues, will excel. In the groundbreaking research conducted by Patterson, Grenny, McMillan and Switzler, summarized in their book *Crucial Confrontations,* it was demonstrated that the ability to confront is key to effective leadership and team building. Those who lacked the ability to confront could not inspire others to perform, they were often viewed as angry, weak or cynical. Their research validates that this skill is vital to cultivate if we want to evolve our relationships both in and out of the workplace.

A Willingness To Be Transparent

Some of us avoid conflict because it requires a willingness to have our own perspectives and behaviors judged and evaluated. Yet, if you look at highly functioning teams, you will notice transparency. Everyone is willing to evaluate and be evaluated. Furthering our progress requires that we are willing to be inspected and our ideas challenged. We should possess thoughtful reasons and validations for our perspective. There is tremendous freedom when we not only demonstrate thoughtful, intentional behaviors and communication, but are also willing to change when better options are identified. This comes with an ability to be comfortable with perspectives that disagree with our own and a willingness to change our minds when it makes sense. Such willingness also supplies the bravery required to pose really eyebrow-raising, counterintuitive, out-of-the-box ideas that can ultimately be truly transformative.

When it comes to authentic and effective communication, it is, as Dr. Sangwan says; "If you can stay put for just a little longer—and get a little comfy with the discomfort—a wonderful new world awaits you." A world where honest communication creates endless possibilities.

Conflict and Personal Bias

We all have our own ideas and viewpoints often creating unconscious and inherent bias. Some biases have never been fully reasoned through, we have just accepted them as so. Bias can occur as a result of family influence, culture, religion and political perspectives that we have adopted without question. Some arise from perceptions of events despite the lack of factual evidence to support our perceptions. Many times, we just go along with the narrative, parroting what we heard. We end up challenging nothing nor fully understanding the issues around those opinions.

Bias originates as a way to categorize and make sense of things. Progress in conflict resolution is hampered if we do not accept bias as a human condition. One of my favorite pearls from Dr. Sangwan's book is the discussion about this very human tendency toward bias:

> "It is essential to understand that difference between objective data and our interpretations. If you know how to navigate this external data, then you can recognize that what you think are facts are actually your observations mixed with your thoughts, beliefs, ideas, and perceptions. There's a big difference! Being able to distinguish different forms of incoming data allows you to make decisions and navigate conflict with ease."

Failing to understand this results in clouded vision. It's not that being biased is wrong, it's a natural human condition, culturally acquired. We are better served if we realize biases exist and impact what we do and how we think—recognizing where and how is the point. Acknowledging we have some inherent blindness makes it easier to consider that we must invite differing viewpoints to continue evolving and avoid the narrowminded conditions which create stagnation and conflict. Unquestioned bias effectively means we end up mired in group think. Our ability to originate and articulate new ideas deteriorates. We find other birds of a feather and flock together, thereby avoiding conflicting viewpoints. While it may be comfortable here, our rigidity has us failing to recognize where there is common ground and any inherent faults we may possess.

Approaching Conversations Constructively

In my own life, I am on the opposite end when it comes to conflict avoidance. Initiating the confrontation is not scary for me. I'm brave that way, it's doing it well that is the challenge. I was fascinated to discover that the reason I didn't do it well had something in common with the conflict avoiders—it was fear. I was fearful that I'm not capable of doing it right and had worries of rejection. That fear causes me to be more defensive and reactive. What we'll launch into next are some of the tools I've gathered to help. Using them continues to improve my ability to navigate conflict more successfully.

I have much greater success when I first speak to factors that we can agree upon and make the effort so others are not left feeling wrong. It's more of an invitation to explore a problem that we solve together. If I approach confrontations without feeling like I have to win or be right and I remain open to other perspectives, I meet with greater success. In fact, the synergy of combining our perspectives can be quite powerful and the end result can be even better than I imagined. I have more than a few stories where people I never thought I would get along with were elevated to great working relationships through this approach.

It is also true that confrontation is not always necessary. It is enough, at times, to know our truth without having to demonstrate a point. We have to ask ourselves what is as stake, if it really matters, or if it is any of our business. Asking ourselves if we are being ego driven or core value driven is necessary. I think it was Will Rogers, that old-time cowboy who used to say this: "Don't ever miss a good chance to shut up."

For the most part, confronting issues stimulates growth. It excites the brain to create other solutions and helps us drill down on what we value most. Our willingness to confront and take part in honest dialogue allows us to increase our understanding of those we engage with, who we are, what we stand for and where we are going. We become a more refined human being and achieve deeper, more fulfilling relationships. The more we practice it, the less scary it becomes. The possibility of being incorrect causes less worry because we are more willing to be flexible and grow.

Blame Sidetracks, Ownership Fast-tracks

Theodore Roosevelt brilliantly said, "If you could kick the person in the pants responsible for most of your trouble, you wouldn't sit for a month." Aren't we often looking for who to kick in the pants when problems arise? It should be a liberation to know then, at least some of time the one responsible is ourselves, an entity under our control. Well that's a relief!

When tragedy strikes or difficulties arise it is a common and very human reaction to search for a place to lay blame. We shout, "Who's responsible for this!" As though we need to tie someone to the stake. No one wants to be the one who was wrong, so we get to work finding whom we can assign that oner- ous responsibility to while simultaneously bolstering how we couldn't possibly be involved. Many of us feel satisfied when we can squarely place blame and passionately articulate all the details of why it belongs there. We dust off our hands with a smug look on our face and say, "Well! I'm certainly glad we got to the bottom of that!" and then walk away thinking the work is done. Is this because we feel vindicated? Superior maybe? Or maybe just relieved that we were not the ones to blame. At the root of this, I believe, is an exaggerated fear of being wrong, as though our own death would surely follow if we were.

Our management of errors, culturally and medically, have historically been primarily focused on individual blame rather than one of taking a larger view. It is much easier to fire or vil- lainize one person or a singular entity than to look big picture and evaluate how our various cultures, systems and practices contributed to the problem. We shy away from that because it feels like we are opening Pandora's box and are overwhelmed by the possibility that we may have to fix a really big problem or that we may indeed have played some part in what went awry. The reality is however, that investing in the big picture will save greater amounts of time in the future and may even save a life in many lines of work. It's important to understand that if one person goes down a wrong road within an established system, then someone else may also.

In the world of aviation accident analysis, now being widely incorporated into medical error analysis, errors are understood to rarely be singular flukes and almost never can be attributed to just one person or circumstance. They are almost without exception a series of errors or omissions with a cast of characters. Like slices of stacked Swiss cheese, every now and then all the holes will line up and an error finds its way through. Each slice of cheese represents various policies and safeguards that, for whatever behavioral, system- or human-related reason, failed in their purpose to prevent the progression of missteps to the point of error. This plays out in catastrophic ways and in small ways in the minutia of life. Take, for example, the spectacular skiing wipeout my husband once had on our first ski trip together in Lake Tahoe, California.

First Swiss cheese hole: My husband is hard of hearing but was too prideful to get hearing aids at the time.

Second Swiss cheese hole: I'm the better skier, he the novice, and I was perhaps a bit too "helpful" in my delivery of instructions so he was tired of my incessant commentary.

Third Swiss cheese hole: I knew he was irritated with me, but still being concerned for his welfare, I warned him in too soft a voice—which was stupid since he can't hear—"Watch out for those *poles* babe, probably a hazard."

Fourth Swiss cheese hole: He, in his annoyance had stopped listening so when I said "Watch out for those *poles*," he heard just another minimal value commentary: "Watch out for the *holes*, blah blah blah. Does she think I'm not bright enough to know I should avoid a *hole*? Good grief!!!"

Final Swiss cheese hole: Off he went at full speed to demonstrate his evolving mastery of the slopes. Whipping past the poles at full tilt, off an eight-foot drop, across a road for snow equipment travel not visible from above, exploding into a mass of ski equipment strewn fifty feet down the hill. After he caught his breath and realizing what had occurred, he yelled, "I thought you said 'Watch out for the holes,' not poles!" Nothing broken, thank God.

Most often errors are a shared responsibility. If we want to fix the cause of a mistake, we have to be willing to look at what part each of us had leading up to the event (by action or failure to act) and how effective our safeguard systems are. As I dissected what happened in Lake Tahoe, I identified the following factors: My husband felt he was "too young" to get hearing aids and that attitude impacted his safety; I came across too bossy which fostered his resistance to listening; I only knew about poles as hazard markers because I was an experienced skier; and finally, I would definitely question the wisdom of using such an ambiguous hazard communication system.

Shifting from our habit of placing blame on individuals takes courage. Being transparent to own our part can be hard to do. It is so much more comfortable to come from an angle of zero responsibility given no one likes to be part of a mistake. We have to get our heads wrapped around the fact that blame is mostly inflammatory and rarely—if ever—moves a team forward toward higher levels of function. Blame brings out defensiveness, it steers us away from accurate accountability, reduces the chance of people stepping up to own their part and is at the root of why practitioners at all levels of medicine may be enticed to not report errors. This discomfort of ownership rises exponentially when the stakes are exceptionally high, as in the arena of medicine and aviation, where lives may be lost. But hello...we're human. Errors occur. It's much better to share in our humanness, at very least acknowledging to the person who made the error that we've made them too. Dissect the event together, stay out of judgment, try to understand how they made the mistake, learn and move on. Everyone benefits from this approach, it provides personal growth, teams are strengthened and patients are safer. This does not mean that we toss out the idea of improvement plans for some, it means that we help others to improve in a supportive way.

The whole blame mentality plays out in other areas of daily life. Sometimes the blame mentality has been established so completely that it becomes how life operates 24/7, whether it is in a marriage, a healthcare staff or relating to the world as a whole. When individuals or groups decide to stop talking, get busy with shaming and avoid confronting issues in a civil and constructive manner and fail to ask the pivotal question "How did this issue evolve and what part did I play in it," we can find ourselves making all kinds of theoretical assumptions and assigning fault in grossly inaccurate ways. In this kind of environment the best-case result will be marginal maintenance of the status quo, and in most cases a gradual deterioration of the team, relationship or perhaps even a country. Evolution to something better is smothered to death by the habit of blame.

When we get in the habit of looking first to our part in an event, whether due to an action or inaction, and own our piece of it (where our "circle of influence" is most effective,) others begin to have confidence that they also can honestly proclaim their part. Even if we are not directly involved in an event, we still have the responsibility to ask ourselves where we could have influenced an outcome. All events arise out of the context of our environments which each of us has, knowingly or unknowingly, contributed to creating. If we do not put forth the effort to make asking questions easy, others will not ask, they will just do, basing those actions on assumptions; or perhaps to avoid being ridiculed for asking about what they don't know.

Do we personally cultivate a collaborative, supportive and mentoring environment? Are we approachable? Do we actively promote a safe environment for patients and coworkers? Do we hold ourselves and others accountable when unhealthy communication dynamics or bullying are at play? Do we stand up for core values? Asking and honestly answering these questions means that we have matured to the point where we comprehend that the "organism" of our work environment is entirely interconnected. No part of it functions independent of the whole. When we get to a place where we are 100% invested in the organism and are always striving in our own small way to support its well-being, we have achieved a level of excellence that brings with it profound results and true satisfaction. When an entire team pulls on the yoke this way, anything is possible. This is how we create work environments that are enviable, a place where people want to be a part of it.

Full disclosure of all factors is also the best place to create an optimal solution. Gratitude and praise for that level of honesty and courage should be expressed and encouraged. As we practice this consistently, full disclosure becomes easier and easier. While unlikely we will create a completely error-free environment, we can reduce the number of mistakes dramatically and powerfully improve our ability to prevent similar mistakes in the future.

On a more intimate level, all relationships are their own organism operating within an environment. Ownership of what we can control (our thoughts, words and actions) also takes practice, deliberate attention and courage. We can all be mentors to be mindful of its importance. It is easy for anyone to have old habits slip through that need correction and new members of a group may need coaching to support this exceptional dynamic.

Sometimes simple apologies are necessary when we miss the mark. "I'm sorry I snapped at you, I was feeling overwhelmed and you got the brunt of it. I hope you will accept my apology and I will try to do better next time." The pitfall of *"You made me mad and that's why I did it"* is pretending that we only have the level of control that a toddler or a hormonal teenager possesses. We can do better than that. Apologies may be hard to do in the beginning, but you will see the more often you own your stuff, the easier it becomes. An added benefit to apologizing is that by necessity—since we all know that apologies only go so far if we continue to repeat the same behavior—we begin to be more aware of our choices and actions. Our ownership grows and we become much more conscious and deliberate in how we handle our emotions and what we think, do and say. With this kind of true ownership we step into *responsiveness,* instead of a *reactive* state and begin choosing how to respond based on desired outcome, rather than simply reacting to our emotions that the behavior of others or our own duress may elicit.

It may not feel comfortable that we are in the position of having to speak to a colleague about an unpleasant subject, but when we do it without blame, with integrity, compassion and thoughtfulness, assuring the person fully comprehends that the focus is a positive outcome for all involved, it is infinitely easier. It may not be comfortable to let a coworker know that her heated phone conversations with her kids at the nurses' station creates an uncomfortable environment for others, but we can do it in a way that is kind, compassionate and honest. It may elicit some embarrassment on the part of the individual, but that can be motivation for learning, and if we are compassionate regarding their discomfort, forward progress can be made. And they will get over it more readily if we genuinely come across as wanting the best for them, are forgiving of their human weakness and avoid assigning shame and blame. Focusing on desired outcomes and their human potential rather than our perceived defects in a person, helps to keep conversations on track rather than sidetracking to the defensive.

Avoid Clouding The Issue

It is equally problematic if we over-soften the issue to the point of muddiness. Our lack of directness leaves too much room for assumption on the receiver's part, they may even think that you really don't care about whether the behavior changes or not.

We often do not know why people are the way they are. Usually, there are a great number of factors that we are likely unaware of. We can only provide feedback or counsel from our perspective of how another's behavior affects us or affects our patients. Providing that feedback with kindness and compassion that is both specific in what has occurred and clear about the change we hope to see, is the best we can offer and will help us productively manage the conversation.

Many of us have a tendency to try to figure other people out, theorizing about what we think is behind the behaviors of another. That's just making up stories. But really, how others live their lives or think about things is out of our control and, frankly, none of our business. The focus is the impact behaviors are having. It is usually not helpful to dig for understanding why other people do what they do. This is their job, and if we butt in uninvited, things can shift to what feels like an intrusive and personal attack. Giving this "why" any headspace will cloud the issue and detract from our effectiveness at communication. Certainly support others if they explain the cause, but if we are in a work situation, make sure it is made clear that blaming something else for their behavior is not what we are after. Ownership, self-control, excellent patient care, better relationships and fostering the greater good is the goal.

Sometimes it may be appropriate to encourage getting some outside help, such as the team's input or the perspective of a counselor, supervisor, or educator when difficulties arises. It also is a point of integrity to redirect when someone comes to you to talk *about* someone. We want to encourage talking *with* the persons involved. In the end, the commitment to self-manage and follow healthy codes of conduct lies with the individual. Helping others to see possibility and their own ability to grow, problem-solve and be successful, is the best gift we can offer.

Healthy Codes Of Conduct

It is appropriate, in any relationship or work environment, to establish and hold ourselves accountable to a code of conduct.

We become far more effective, both individually and in how we function as a team, when we commit to managing our own emotions, feelings and behaviors, and commit to correcting things when we get off track. This means not only speaking with respect, it means we are respectful in spite of our likes or dislikes as they pertain to others. It means we are committed and willing to talking it out when we get off track. But I would ask you, is this ideal really supported in our day to day workplace? Sure we all attend orientations that speak to this, but do we as coworkers and does our leadership make that code of conduct a living, breathing thing? This level of ownership is where the powerhouse of cultural change lies.

Organizational codes of conduct are usually imposed externally on employees. Little effort is made to do the work that results in the internal motivation to practice them. These codes are also often inconsistently applied by the leadership. If leadership is not exemplifying them well in their personal and professional lives, it is not likely to be fostered in the workplace or any other place of influence they may have. Codes of conduct can in some places become weaponized and used as an tool of punishment as opposed to a tool of growth if we forget the importance of avoiding shame and blame. This is precisely why codes of conduct have to be fostered from within if we have any hope of making our workplaces where dream job environments can happen. Individuals have to be mentored as to the hows and whys of civility and supporting others. Practice of it has to be actively cultivated. Individuals who are not getting it must be held accountable to doing their own work to get there. These days most organizations have Employee Assistance Programs (EAPs) which are great places to foster this kind of internal shift.

Healthy codes of conduct also relate to using what is called "accountability language." Its application is effective because it makes clear what's what. A familiar example is the practice of sticking to "I statements" when communicating the essence of a situation from our own point of view. This makes clear to the listener that this is *our* personal perspective. It places us in ownership of our own thoughts, perceptions and emotions.

Sharing perspective clearly with accountable language also helps the listener grasp that we are not presuming everyone sees a situation as we do. If we use the word "you," discussions can be perceived as an accusation that may or may not be true, arousing defensiveness or wounding others. "You were very nasty with me" is quite hurtful to a kind-hearted person who, at the moment of interaction referred to, was actually just feeling stressed and overwhelmed with the circumstances.

Expressing clearly how things impacted us and owning it as our perception of events leaves room for dialogue and the opportunity to set things right. "Hey Cheryl, I wanted to check in with you. Are you upset with me? I was feeling like you may be since our last interaction seemed so tense from my perspective" is far better than labeling the behavior as "nasty." Or worse yet, to gossip with others about "how nasty Cheryl is." Much of the time a person's poor behavior actually has nothing to do with us, yet we most often assume that it does.

Accountable language also helps with simple clarity. Using "you" can become confusing when what we actually mean is "I," forcing others to ask the question, did you mean me or were you talking about yourself? When a friend says, "You know how you feel when you're talking to your boss and you get all nervous?" That can be confusing when what they really are talking about is their own feelings and responses. It would be far clearer if we were to say, "When I talk to my boss, I feel very nervous." That is a personal statement about our personal reality, which does not assume another's personal experience matches our own.

Using the term "you" instead of "I" is also a bit of a trick that we use to distance ourselves from uncomfortable ownership of our behaviors or, as in the statement above, the fact that some get nervous around the boss. Using "I" causes our brains to process the information differently. It facilitates owning our own experiences and behaviors as pertaining to us, demonstrates clarity that this is our own perspective and acknowledges that this perspective may not necessarily be what the listener experiences. Using "I" also places us squarely in the driver's seat should a change in perspective be needed.

A Word On Judging Others

It's not uncommon to dole out careless judgment about others without any factual basis. Having a healthy code of conduct should consider gossip as discourteous. While we need to exercise some judgment about others to be safe and make important decisions, doing so without validating fact can get us way off base. Being judgmental of others is rarely helpful in creating a trusting, healthy work environment. Tending to our own house, making sure we are acting with integrity, doing what we are supposed to do and being respectful is the extent of our job, unless of course we are the boss who has the job of gathering facts and making decisions.

How far we can be off track in our judgments is well demonstrated by a story Steven Covey relates. He was riding a subway sitting next to a man with several children, each of whom were running around, being loud and playing as young children do. The man was sitting quietly, saying nothing to his children as they bumped into passengers and collected stares. As Steven's annoyance grew about the man's "poor parenting skills," he finally said to the man—unable to conceal his irritation—"Sir! Can you *please* get your children under control?" The comment seemed to startle the man and he responded in a sad, hesitant voice, "Oh...I'm so sorry. We just left the hospital where my wife finally lost her battle with cancer. Come children, please sit with daddy."

It's human to interpret circumstances from our own experiential context. Our assumptions and beliefs create inherent blind spots when we are unaware of this tendency. There is a useful saying in the personal development world; "All judgment is self-judgment," meaning we most easily recognize both positive and negative characteristics in others because they are familiar, because we have them ourselves. We may have learned to moderate those tendencies, but having had them makes us experts in recognizing these characteristics outside ourselves. If you find yourself particularly critical of another, take stock of where you may have something in your own life similar to what you are judging in the other person about. It can go a long way toward humbling our ideas about things, fostering an open and compassionate approach toward others and a more curious mind about what may really be going on with someone, rather than assuming we have all the answers.

Communication with others, the subtlety of blame and the power of true ownership are complex subjects. To truly improve in this way is a time investment that successful individuals prioritize. Some of us are naturals; others of us have to work harder for it and all of us will miss the mark at least on occasion. We first have to put in the work to understand ourselves, take ownership of our values, our biases and perspectives before we can effectively communicate without blame. I would recommend investing time to read Dr. Sangwan's "I-5 Communication Steps," outlined in *Talk Rx,* practice the Awareness Wheel For Effective Communication or use the other resources to enhance your skill that I have on my website, cjsnow.net. I think you will find the reading both intriguing and helpful. Everyone has barriers that can trip us up. But time invested in learning to be an effective communicator is critical to the creation of a life we can be proud of. We simply cannot create an environment of self-motivation, accountability and excellence unless we build a culture of trust that evolves from authentic, effective communication. Life is a shared experience and our healthy interdependence is necessary if we want to achieve our dreams.

If you take away one concept from this segment, let it be this: Have curiosity about what really happened (avoiding assumptions or assigning blame) and understand that fears and feelings of being overwhelmed are often at the root of bad behavior.

Understanding this assists us to depersonalize the behaviors of others. Our responses will naturally become freer of blame, thus more appropriate, compassionate, and positively directed. Taking full ownership of our experiences makes us better stewards of our own personal growth. It helps us avoid the shackling effects of shame when we stay stuck in blaming ourselves for poor choices, or conversely, stuck in anger if we blame others for our circumstances. Hold on to this bit of understanding and you will be making tremendous strides in your own development as well as your communication and connection with others.

··· 10 ···

Fostering Competence
Is Everyone's Job

"The secret of freedom lies in educating people, whereas the secret of tyranny is in keeping them ignorant."

Maximillian Robespierre

INCOMPETENCE. IT'S A harsh word that we can throw out to describe others who don't measure up to our expectations. And yes, it is another form of blame and oppression to apply such labels. I give it its own chapter because I hear it so often in the healthcare industry. Passing out this judgment is holding us back, limiting our potential and damaging our inventory of people.

What strikes me most is the insensitivity because it has a tone of finality, which implies a lack of possibility to ever be better. It also has the potential to create devastating and lasting emotional wounds. Those painful sorts of memories can burn for a long time and are, more often than not, less about incompetence and more about a lack of experience or proper guidance. Or, perhaps, that hiring practices are not what they should be. Think about it. It is truly rare that a person will, no matter how much training, correction or education you throw at them, remain incompetent. Most simply have never been taught, or they are too afraid to ask for help because they are in an environment that is unforgiving about "not knowing." If we own and correct those pieces, we can make progress.

We all can appreciate there are times when we find ourselves in the category of "innocently ignorant," which I like to call "ignocence." It's not an excuse, we just sometimes have yet to get the memo that informs us. Those with their integrity squared away are internally driven to correct such deficits, but if an "ignocent" lacks this kind of drive, as a professional we are obligated to assist in inspiring growth and make visible the benefits of doing so—those we serve depend on it.

This is not a chapter about weeding out the unworthy. It is a chapter dealing with the creation of competence, and differentiating between those who are "ignocent," and those who are not a good fit for the job or lack the drive to rise above their insufficiencies after we've addressed them. Some may fall into the category of just not caring about a job being done well, but such a label should not be applied without investigation.

We in the medical sector tend to quickly pass judgment on others' performance and sometimes do not even think about asking for the facts. We frequently just assume that we have the essential details straight and fail to consider that big picture perspective we discussed in the last chapter. This propensity to carelessly pass judgment and apply the label of "incompetent" is why we have the long-standing reputation of "eating our young."

All of us have made mistakes, sometimes because we simply just did not know better or perhaps because we failed to follow instructions. Maybe the instructions did not make sense to us or we allowed distractions to interfere. Possibly our error was created by the pressures of the job that have us hurtling through the day at warp speed so that we can get it all done. Perhaps we believed that skipping a step wouldn't be that big a deal. Maybe we were lax in education and keeping ourselves current. Whatever the reason, mistakes happen and competence can come into question.

Some of us think, when hearing of another's mistake, "thank goodness that wasn't me!" Even those at high levels of expertise have occasions where they err, sometimes because having a lot of experience can evolve to complacency. The discomfort in owning an error is unpleasant, but it will be a recurrent human experience that we are better served to embrace rather than resist or deny. Owning our part, reviewing what happened and learning from it is the most professional thing we can do. We will have greater pride when we execute this level of integrity and accountability. If we are in the sphere of a person who errored, the most professional thing we can do is to visibly support that person to learn and grow. When that becomes a visible behavior in a workplace, trust builds, competition lessens, mentorship becomes the norm and people generally become happier to be part of our team.

Medicine compounds the risk of making mistakes by its necessary and continual evolution. Often what was gospel yesterday is ignorant folly today. This having to keeping up with the latest and greatest creates its own prevailing anxiety in medicine, where we all hope that when we go to work today we are up to speed about proper care. No one likes to be thought of as ignorant, but it is an occasional event for everyone in a field that is ever evolving. Because of this, there are bound to be instances where we butt up against unknowns where ignorance-based errors occur.

True incompetence is rare. Yet we as providers, in our quick-to-judge mentality, (a quality that can both save a life and be a curse of temperament), can jump to conclusions that a person's incompetence is at the root of their error. No wonder nurses, doctors and host of other professions hide errors. It does not feel safe to own them.

Great leaders habitually think big picture, as discussed in our last chapter, and are best served when naturally curious about the root cause of things. True leaders instinctively assume they have much to learn about the facts surrounding circumstances and are not afraid to look at how their own actions have directly or indirectly contributed to circumstances. Mitigating perceived incompetence then, is first about making sure we have done everything we could to assist others to be competent, and this holds true whether we are in a formal position of leadership or not.

Generating excitement to always be learning can be challenging. Most of my experience with annual competency training where nurses practice with equipment and skills we don't often use, has been one of a large, collective groan. "Again? Already???" It has not been one of excitement about learning or honing skills. Interestingly, I have observed the teaching staff even buying in to that attitude too. "OK," they say with a big sigh that matches the staff's, "Sorry we have to have you come in for this. Will do our best to make it as painless as possible." It has been somewhat rare when I saw a person excited about the opportunity to get a tune-up. At my last long-term employer, it was decided that a new education team should be formed made up of front-line personnel. I had the privilege to join that team. One of the first things we dealt with was this negativity about training. We decided to deliberately shift to modeling excitement over learning and promoted a message to pursue excellence in practice. Our modeling and enthusiasm for learning was recognized and appreciated. A gradual shift in perspective occurred. The experience was perceived as worthwhile and essential to remaining competent, confident and capable. Can we say "Be the change we wish to see?" Yup we did.

When I was a flight nurse, we had competencies twice a year called Clinical Training Labs, held in a Sim Man lab, which employs a mechanical patient that gives as real an experience as possible. These were conducted in the presence and under the direction of our physician medical director and regional nurse educator. Each nurse-paramedic team attended these as a duo, in our flight suits with all our usual gear to simulate our daily reality. In the spring we focused on pediatrics and obstetrics, and in the fall on adult medicine. We had four case scenarios where we were expected to manage care according to protocol. The experience lasted three to four hours.

The cases presented were gleaned from actual care situations where a flight crew either managed a case brilliantly or made some care choices that were not optimal. In either case, it was thought the learnings from these cases would benefit all crews, so they set about ensuring that everyone had the benefit of the learning. Most us newly hired were nervous about the prospect of being scrutinized at this level. Eventually, we all came to understand that we were being provided an extraordinary opportunity and were expected to be learning in this safe and supportive environment. It was the first time that I was thoroughly supported and held accountable for the knowledge provided in the protocols. My job was to put forth my best and be open to learning. Each training session then became an exciting event where I was challenged and enjoyed the learning and the teamwork. This "always learning" culture was the foundation of our solid reputation for consistently providing exceptional care and one that I have carried forward in my career where I hoped to facilitate a culture like that for every workplace.

To inspire excellence at a high level, competence must be positively discussed, cultivated and passionately pursued. A visible bar has to be set. We are far better served by creating an environment of consistently learning rather than one that ferrets out "incompetence." Most importantly, this same principle has to be actively cultivated at all levels of an organization. Formal leaders can't just be installed, they have to be actively cultivated and continually supported to grow in their leadership skills.

Competency is greatly enhanced by a clear set of core values specific to the mission intended, coupled with a visibly pursued ideal of being the best. Beyond the organized policies, procedures and training, when people are clear about the organization's core values, they are provided with a foundation to make good decisions. Decisions consistent with the standards and culture, even when situations don't squarely fit a policy or procedure.

During my time as a flight nurse it was a career-first that I actually knew by heart and understood the core values stated in my organization's mission statement. Not only did it state what I believed was at the heart of medicine, but it was referred to over and over again in our training and was demonstrated by my superiors and senior crewmembers and administrators in their actions. Our mission statement was a living thing with tentacles reaching all the aspects of who we were. This is how leadership actively drove and supported the incredible culture they had created. It also made decision making at the front line much easier. When we as a crew had to make decisions that didn't fit any protocol or seemed to beg for a move counter to what policy or protocol outlined, we simply went down the mission statement's core values to see if our proposed action fit and was the best thing for the patient given our circumstances. Those were the simple but powerful constructs and the final, bottom line, decision making factors. Our competent decision making came from a clarity about organizational goals and ideals, as well as the facts and circumstances. Such a living mission statement gives caregivers the confidence and strength to do what needs to be done, even when situations are not listed in the playbook.

Embracing Our Weak Spots Is Not Easy, So Be Patient

Everyone will always have learning to do, but not always do we welcome that idea. It would be a mistake to assume that once we get experience or get into positions of leadership that we "have arrived" in some way that makes us exempt. Uphill battles do occur, so patience is required—both for others and ourselves.

Gentleness and coaxing are required at times to overcome the natural resistance that arises when there is a need for improvement. I for one am deeply grateful to those who were patient with me and hung in there until I "got it." Try to compassionately remember that resistance to growth is usually rooted in a fear of being discovered as inadequate in some way. The best we can offer is a safe environment that acknowledges we all have these learning edges, or those places where we reach the limits of ability or of what we know. Embracing that reality is what gives us the courage to stretch a little bit further.

We all have occasions during our careers where we are not exactly on sure ground. Nurturing the perspective where a place of not knowing is viewed as an exciting place of learning can create powerful shifts, both internally and in workplace culture. In that space we are open and can move away from any fears we may be holding on to regarding our lack. It puts a whole new spin on creating competence when approached this way. When we are fully honest about what we may be lacking, it's not only a relief from having to pretend we're better than we are, it's worthy of respect. It strengthens our commitment to what we value—being honest and committed to continually improve and serve our patients well.

As I said, hopeless incompetence is a rarity. The work lies in supporting people to be their best and learning to embrace where there is more to do. It is unlikely that a medical professional arrives on your unit without enough smarts to provide good care. It is just too hard to get through the education and licensing process without having at least a modicum of intelligence. Focusing on improvement and contributing where we can, even in small ways, will give us a more competent staff member and we will likely gain their loyalty for having invested in them. And it is not just the educator's or administrator's responsibility to provide a positive learning environment. All of us are meant to cultivate competence through mentoring when opportunities arise. We owe it to the people we care for and the organization we work for. In spite of these efforts, we may arrive at a conclusion that the person is unwilling to learn or the line of work they are in is not a good fit. At least we can send them off in good conscience, knowing we have done our best to instill confidence within them to find where they do fit and can contribute in an excellent and satisfying way. Anyone who enters a career of service deserves that.

··· 11 ···

You Are Not Your Career

"Taking time to live life will only inspire your work."

Unknown

EARLY IN MY career, I was fully identified with the noble pride in our profession. I used to view myself first as a nurse whose name is Carolyn. Now I am Carolyn, who has the good fortune to be a nurse *and a whole bunch of other stuff too*. One secret of a happy life is having what we do for a living and who we are as individuals in balanced perspective, with all aspects of our identities attended to so they are full and complete.

Part of the heaviness we all feel at times in our profession can be related, in part at least, to the perspective that our careers are the bulk of what validates our self-worth. And it's not just medicine holding this perspective. How many parties have you been to where shortly after someone gets your name, they ask what you do for a living?

We all need non-career places in our lives where we can take a deep breath and just be. Without these alternate dimensions the difficulties of many jobs can be suffocating to the human spirit. While being a nurse or other healthcare professional is a recognizable anchor and source of pride, it will become the anchor that drags us down when we're facing the more challenging parts of the job or are having difficulties in our careers. Without other places to go when we need to put the load of caregiving down for a while—and I mean places that don't involve a bottle of booze or a TV remote—we can be drowned by the sheer weight of the pressures.

In our early careers, often before we have families of our own, the pride of having such a noble profession is intoxicating, particularly if you choose a challenging avenue of practice. The timing of it varies depending on the intensity of your work venue, but I have noticed in the critical care arena that the glamour and enthusiasm we apply to the job lasts about two to five years before the varnish is worn off enough that cynicism begins to creep in. By then we've been made clearly aware of our own human flaws and inadequacies and have endured the less than glamourous portions of the job over and over again. We may have been rattled by challenging experiences, or may be asking if we really like what we do. Here is where the first components of burnout can start laying down a foundation. This most often evolves into blaming others or circumstances for our discomfort. Enabling this perspective are the readily available comrades who will validate all the reasons for a cynical perspective and endorse beliefs that we are victims of innumerable injustices. This perspective can soon become our habit where we then habitually validate and perpetuate them, sometimes for the rest of our careers. As the years go by and our habits of cynicism entrench, what follows is a diminishing satisfaction and engagement.

This habit of negativity has a cascade of effects. Part of the reality of becoming a healthcare provider is that we promise and commit to offer the best care, to save lives and to do no harm, a much greater responsibility than most folks have in other careers. If we begin slipping in our commitment and fail to wholeheartedly fill it as a result of our perceived complaints, our ever-present better selves cannot forgive the transgression. Consciously or unconsciously, we become aware that we have broken our word, find it detestable, and our own self-loathing may begin. Not everyone will have the self-awareness to recognize this, but the effects of self-loathing are far reaching. In that mental state we also are likely to become toxic to our environment, dragging it down with the weight of our negativity.

It is natural to struggle. The challenge is having the ability to recognize when we drift from what we idealized ourselves to be, determine its cause and set about fixing it. We can feel shame about the fact that we struggle and become disheartened when we find out how imperfect we are, how we can fall short or are somehow becoming the burnt-out provider we swore we would never be.

If my Grandfather had a flaw, it would have been his over-weighted sense of identity with being a physician. Though he had a lot of interests such as gardening, history and travel, when he retired, he was devastated. It was a very sad thing to watch him deteriorate rapidly after leaving the profession. He had earned the time to just enjoy life but had trouble doing so without the patient/doctor relationships he enjoyed so much and the prestige he had always been shown as a doctor. I've had to do my own work in wrapping my head around leaving the critical care nurse arena. A part of my world was ending and I grieved. Being in a sweet-spot in all stages of our life requires balancing our careers with elements that offer us differing identities and a different type of satisfaction *outside of the job.* This is part of how we avoid lingering in this funky place of feeling stuck, being overwhelmed by our career demands, or feeling like our life is over when we retire.

Many can find a sense of career balance in raising a family, but I would encourage those to also find an undertaking that is independent of family, something that you can call your own. Woodworking, gardening, photography, martial arts, artistry, cooking, going to the gym—many things creative and physical will provide you with an outlet and venue to accomplish where the stakes are not as risky and the burden of responsibility is less. It will give you an avenue to relate to yourself in a different way, to see yourself as accomplished in ways other than a healthcare professional or a parent.

Every naturally sustaining life form has opposing forces that create balance within the organism essential to its survival. We can no more do without acids in the body than we can do without bases to make the life-sustaining pH we require. This is precisely why those of us in high intensity environments—which the majority of healthcare qualifies for in this age of budget cuts and doing more with less while we constantly raise the bar of what we are expected to know and do—have to find ways to engage in low-stress activities. Television, video games and shopping may be sources of relaxation at times, but they won't offer us much in the way of rejuvenation because we are not creating anything out of our own imagination or the kind of lasting, pleasant and relaxing emotions experienced when we engage in a memorable activity or spend time in nature. Undertakings that have a creative dimension, or something we have an emotional connection to, or perhaps engage us in a physically demanding way, all feed us in necessary ways. Make time for those activities, make precious memories and make it a priority! This is how we will have staying power in a high-stress career.

If you want a high functioning healthcare team that is resistant to burnout, mentor your coworkers in doing things that help create balance. Share your stories of these activities and celebrate with others the different parts of their lives that make them more than a good healthcare provider. Work together to create some fun, creative or competitive activities. Get to know each other as whole people rather than just job titles. As we begin to see the multiple dimensions of people, we understand that they are complex and unique in their own way, we discover more common ground, and we have a greater ability to connect with and respect them.

Peace naturally finds its way into a well-balanced life. If we are experiencing a lack of it in our lives, the simple remedy is to make time for something we truly love, not just entertained by. Make a list of activities that fulfil you at the deepest level and prioritize time for them often. I promise you...it's like having your own bag of magic tricks for manifesting a life that you love.

··· 12 ···

Burnout, The Code Blue Of A Career

"Burnout is nature's way of telling you you've been going through the motions [and] your soul has departed; you're a zombie, a member of the walking dead, a sleepwalker."

Sam Keen

UGH...NOT A FLATTERING picture is it? If we don't apply some good CPR here, death of our spirits will surely follow.

Burnout is a funny thing. It can be temporary, like the kind we get when working too much to pay off Christmas debt, or we can get stuck in it for years. Sometimes we can be oblivious to the fact that we've landed there. Most of us hate to admit that we have it. The litmus test is simple: if the work you do has serious gaps of fun, joy or satisfaction, you're burnt out. Even if you have never felt burned out, you will no doubt encounter others who are, or may find yourself there eventually.

Burnout is essentially the result of an imbalance in or mismanagement of our internal environment, because this is the wellspring where life's joys come from and where we process our experiences. We forget, or fall out of practice with, the ability to be resourceful or create for ourselves those experiences, feelings and perspectives that once gave us satisfaction and fulfillment. It may be that we spend too much time working or have failed to cultivated the necessary dimensions that validate we are more than our careers. Perhaps we have placed too much emphasis on things that don't meet our needs (the superficial/materialistic elements); have forgotten the joy of curiosity, of learning; are maybe stuck in a perspective of being victimized; or in a place where we see our lives as limited and without options. In burnout we tend to disconnect from others, (I think because we feel ugly in this place and instinctually know we are somewhat repugnant,) we feel alone and unhappy. We may believe it's "just the job," but burnout is like spilled milk. It continues to spread out, contaminating the rest of our lives and how we experience it. Common threads in burnout are a sense of feeling trapped, having little or no control over our experience and that circumstances are to blame for making us what we are...burned out and searching for light at the end of a tunnel.

If we chose to ignore this internal dilemma, that light will be an oncoming train. The cost will be our health and well-being, maybe even our livelihood or those we love. Happiness will be elusive and our ability to be successful will diminish. We can become so fixated on our current distorted beliefs and perspectives we forget about our ability to change those perspectives. We blame, maintain that we are victimized by circumstances and hold on to the belief that someone or something is the origin of our feelings and experience. Conveniently, it is easier to buy in to this way of thinking, because we do not have to take any ownership or responsibility for our experience of discontent.

So here's the really good news: *we are 100% responsible for our internal experience in response to events! If we manage our internal environment, positive experience will follow.* Yep, it's a mind-blower, but no matter how much I initially resisted this idea, I can now say it is without doubt true. We own it, we have control. At least it is a place we can do something about, within our circle of influence and a skill we can learn just as we have learned other things. Take heart, there actually is light at the end of this tunnel.

Don't think of this as your fault, just be compassionate for your humanness. It really is a relief to know we have the ability to control our thoughts, feelings and reactions to circumstances. It is in understanding this at the deepest level that we can support ourselves to rediscover our joy in caregiving, in our workplaces and for the other things in our lives. If we step out of blaming others for our discontent and begin managing how we respond to the events in our lives, we begin creating the life we want.

"Beginning with the end in mind" is a great place to start this process. Clearly visualizing what we want our life to look like and how we want it to feel, fosters a mindfulness about our part in its creation. To this end, I again recommend at least a daily three-to-five-minute meditation of sorts. Closing your eyes, envision your ideal life. What attitudes and feelings will you have? How will your relationships be? What do you look like when you are living in that vision of your ideal self? What facial expressions does the world around you see on your face? Make it as real as possible. Some of us find it helpful to create a vision board with pictures of what we envision. I myself have found this to be greatly helpful. I find that when I do this daily visualization consistently, my sharpened mindfulness helps me understand how I shape my own attitudes, my positive or negative perspectives and I can better manage how I interpret things. As we begin operating from this more aware and positive way of being, we tend to attract and recognize more positive things and people into our lives. We also see more clearly our own connection to the whole. It is as Macy and Johnstone observed in their book, *Active Hope:* "By refreshing our sense of belonging in the world, we widen the web of relationships that nourishes us and protects us from burnout."

Building this type of personal ownership and connection to others is a life's work, and creates a sort of armor that protects us from the wearing-down effects of hardship. Like any new habit, it takes practice to respond in a more deliberate manner to our experiences. The more we practice stepping into that way of operating, the more we see that it can be achieved in any set of circumstances.

If you're doubtful about this concept, consider the empirical documentary efforts by Viktor Frankl, an Austrian neurologist and psychiatrist. His remarkable observations of human experience and behaviors came from internment in Nazi concentration camps. He personally endured horrifying torture and loss of family, including his pregnant wife. He wrote about that experience in *Man's Search for Meaning*, a compelling manuscript that has sold over 10 million copies. What he learned in surviving that extreme experience is that a human's mind is the last and ultimate refuge. "Everything can be taken from a man but one thing: the last of the human freedoms—to choose one's attitude in any given set of circumstances, to choose one's own way." In his book he says that when we are no longer able to change a situation, we are challenged to change ourselves. It is the decision to adapt in a positive way and remain connected to others that leaves our psyche intact where joy can still be experienced. "Life," Viktor says, "is never made unbearable by circumstances, but only by a lack of [personal] meaning and purpose." This meaning and purpose, he determined, was based on a positive vision of the future and our interrelatedness.

Most of us just fall into burnout without an awareness of it actually occurring. We just make the observation one day, "I am sooooo burnt!" You may be experiencing it right now. I certainly have spent some time there and can still fall back into it when my life is out of balance, usually from being over-committed and working too much. We may also be on the other end of the equation where we have an appreciation of the sacredness of what we do, are feeling a little self-righteous about it, and throw out disapproving observations about others. "She's so burnt out," we might remark of a colleague, "she should really move on if she hates it so much." Our quick and harsh judgments of others are just another way to feel better about ourselves, what we've accomplished and how we are of value—if only by the comparison. And if you'll notice, the folks making such judgements are often not any happier than their burnt-out colleagues. Unfortunately, this self-righteous perspective essentially excludes those experiencing burn out from the self-righteous circle. These two camps effectively perpetuate each other's misery in a sort of messed-up symbiosis.

Those of us feeling judgmental should consider for a moment, what if that burnt-out behavior is coming from a provider feeling defeated, inadequate or disheartened beneath whatever behaviors they display? They may have lost sight of their meaning and purpose and how they contribute to something important. In that state, they cannot see a way to change their attitude just as the self-righteous cannot find compassion when they thoughtlessly judge.

Perhaps we should be asking ourselves, what could I do to encourage my burnt-out colleagues? How can I support them in seeing things from a different perspective? Where can I acknowledge their contributions? Talking with and supporting each other in this way can be powerful, connecting and truly liberating. We all go to dark places on occasion. Why not help each other out of it and be grateful when someone tries to help us out of it?

Allowing ourselves to stay stuck in negativity places us at a clear disadvantage. In the field of Positive Psychology, multiple studies validate what is called "the happiness advantage," which, among other things, inoculates us from burnout. These studies focus on people who tested as happier than the average person and studied them to determine how they experience life differently. What the study validated is that the *lens* through with which we view realities shape us rather than the reality itself. The studies show that by changing the lens through which our minds view reality, not only can we change our degree of happiness, we can change educational and business outcomes. The findings also noted that even when we know the external circumstance of an individual's life, we can only predict their long-term happiness with a 10% accuracy, suggesting the individual's viewpoint has the largest influence. This clearly validates that our long-term happiness is predicted not by our external world, but by how our mind processes experiences and circumstances.

Additionally of interest is that IQ has been determined to predict a mere 25% of job success. Optimism levels, social support and the ability to see difficulty as a challenge instead of a threat—these have far more ability to predict job success. Companies are taking notice and interviews are incorporating an assessment of these as part of the job skill package.

Here's how I put this principle to work. I started a new job a few years ago that was not my usual emergency type work I was accustomed to, so it was difficult for me to be somewhat inept as I struggled to get the hang of things. Most of my new coworkers were kind and supportive, but a few brought lots of judgement and wanted me to be sure I knew I was the new kid on the block and not their equal in this venue. Their habits of negativity were tough to be around. A couple coworkers that I quickly became friends with let me know they saw this and didn't approve.

It was easy to polarize into and an "us against them," because my new friends had been living under this tyranny and were tired of it. One afternoon when visiting one of these friends, we got to talking about how this "us against them" didn't really emulate what we value. A smile crept across my face, "What?" my friend asked. "Well, I was just thinking that maybe we should form a gang of sorts, we can call ourselves 'Commandos Of Positivity, the C.O.P.', where our tag line is C.O.P. an attitude!" We all laughed out loud and started discussing how positivity can change environments.

The next day I left a note on her computer which read, "C.O.P. an attitude!" This began the deliberate deployment of positive responses in the face of negative behaviors. I was also mindful of maintaining positive thoughts about the negative people, making sure I did my best to steer clear of being harshly judgmental, being mad at them or holding on to resentment for their treatment of me. So began our empirical testing of "If you don't like what you're getting, look at what you're giving." You know what? Our experience began to improve even though the troublesome people remained as they were. Slowly at first, but the movement was palpable and began creating an environment where we enjoyed it more than before. Supporting each other to be happy and positive was powerful!

There's also a neurochemical basis for the "happiness advantage." A positive lens through which we view things causes dopamine to flood into our system, making us not only happier, it turns on every learning center of our brain. Evidence shows that we are significantly more efficient, make better choices and make more accurate diagnoses when we are in a positive state than we do when we are negative, neutral or stressed. Intelligence, creativity and energy levels all rise. In this positive state, research shows that our performance improves somewhere between 19% and 31%.

Our work lies in retraining our brains to be in a positive state more often than not. Studies show that activities practiced as little as two minutes a day, twenty one days in a row can create change. Activities such as the visualization meditation I suggested earlier is one way to make progress, but there are many, many others. A practice of naming three new things a day (avoiding repeats) that we are grateful for teaches our brain to scan for the positive, both large and small like the delicious cappuccino we had. Journaling or focused reflection about a positive event allows us to relive the positive emotions associated with the experience (here come those natural "feel good" chemicals!) When we do these things, the emotions overflow into other parts of life. Meditation techniques and the exercises above all help our brains get over our culturally-induced ADD that's created by our multitasking in an over-stimulating world. Studies show we accomplish more in this positive state of calmness.

We all know that physical exercise releases endorphins that naturally produce positive feelings of well-being. So does offering random acts of kindness, praising or thanking even just one person a day all have shown to increase positivity. Through these sorts of actions we can ultimately increase our own level of happiness and produce ripples of happiness around us. During Frankl's time in Auschwitz, these are precisely some of the things he did to survive.

The Shackling Effects Of Victim Mentality

Preventing and extracting ourselves from burnout also requires we get a handle on our sense of victimization and the subtle ways in which we allow it. Remaining stuck there is costly to our overall success and toxic to the human spirit. Steve Maraboli says it this way:

> "The victim mindset dilutes the human potential. By not accepting personal responsibility for our circumstances, we greatly reduce our power to change them. Stop validating your victim mentality. Shake off your self-defeating drama and embrace your innate ability to recover and achieve."

If you want a more satisfying existence, one more impervious to the trials, tribulations and major events in life, start by understanding what "victim mentality" is, how we unwittingly allow circumstances to define our experiences, and what perspectives make us free to create our own happiness.

Many of you may have familiarity with the term "victim mentality." I think it's fair to say that many of us save its meaning only for the overtly obvious cases of it. But victimness can be subtle. We ignore its nuances so we don't have to make that uncomfortable step forward to see how it may be showing up in our lives and holding us back. Don't feel alone in this; most of us feel a little unsettled when we probe the possibility. Just take a deep breath, be open, and consider the potentials that arise when you choose to be free of it.

Like any building site, we have to get to stable ground before a foundation can be placed and we have to build that foundation solidly and protect it. If we don't, no matter how wonderful and spectacular a structure we build, it will remain vulnerable. Similarly, the stability of a non-victim/full-ownership mentality is rock solid. If victimization has a chance to take root some-where, the impact can be devastating. Like a root, it can grow ever so slowly and be powerful enough to disrupt the strongest concrete. This is why I want us to dive into its subtleties and how it shows up. It's a "know thy enemy" strategy.

Certainly in the USA it is a societal norm to be in the habit of victimization and we're not alone. We hold other people and circumstances responsible for how we experience life, and in doing so the expectation is that someone outside ourselves has to resolve it. It is, of course, easier this way; to act as though and believe that we are innocent and suffering and it's more sympa-thy-inducing from those also living as victims. In victim mode, we take no ownership for our response to the outside world and the choices we make. When we adopt this perspective we essentially become our own jailers. We place our own shackles and begin to believe we are prisoners of events, people, things and circumstances with no power to make positive influential choices.

Viktor Frankl made the following profound observation about his internment in Hitler's concentration camps:

> "A human being is not one thing among others; things deter-mine each other, but man is ultimately self-determining. What he becomes—within the limits of endowment and envi-ronment—he has made out of himself. In the concentration camps, for example, in this living laboratory and on this test-ing ground, we watched and witnessed some of our comrades behave like swine while others behaved like saints. Man has both potentialities within himself; which one is actualized depends on decisions but not on conditions."

Imagine the freedom we find when we choose to act in ways we admire rather than in ways we do not. Stepping into full accountability for our own life experience means we are free to act, in spite of our contextual circumstances, and free to choose how we will view and experience our lives.

Life will never stop providing circumstances and people who challenge our ability to choose actions, thoughts and deeds that work toward the positive. Living our lives in "responsive mode" instead of "reactive mode" takes clear intention to do so and practice—practice—practice. Just like the way we study, practice, and memorize the elements of treatment for disease, we have to study the motivations behind our own behaviors, set clear intentions to create the life we want and routinely practice doing so with a high degree of awareness. Operating at this level of commitment keeps us free and independent.

One way I incorporate this type of intentionality and ownership is by utilizing my drive time. When working, it was my routine to drive the thirty-five minutes with the radio off, thinking about what I want to create that day, how things in general are going, what sort of learning edges (places of difficulty) I'm working on, and where I can apply my strengths. This engages me in the act of creating what I want, rather than reacting to whatever comes my way. It helps me grasp that I always have choice in how I respond and interpret things. *I get to decide!* Power previously given to circumstances when in the victim mode, dissipates.

When I focus on what I can control (myself) and stop wishing I could make other people behave differently or change those things out of my control, I extract myself from the drama of being a hapless victim. I write the script for how I experience the day. By doing so I get the satisfaction of having excelled in my new-found skill of mastery over my internal environment, and I can contribute in a more effective way. I may leave work at the end of the day not having achieved all I had set out to do, but the practice of putting forth my best effort toward a positive experience is hugely satisfying.

Let's explore the victim mentality in one of its subtler forms. Many of us choose clinical care because we want to be needed, to save lives, or be the one to make a difference in the lives of our patients. These are all nobly intended and made with a generosity of heart which I admire. The problem is that by romanticizing our roles and clinging to end results, we expect— at some level in our psyche—that our purpose will somehow be validated by recurring successful outcomes and appreciation. We may intellectually understand we cannot save every life, alleviate all suffering, nor will all patients and families be grateful for our efforts, but the point is we may create the idea in our heads that fulfilment is contingent on outside results. While a result may be an influencing factor, it certainly is not the determining factor of job satisfaction.

When we have an expectation that we will be acknowledged or appreciated, or that our efforts will prevail for the positive because they are well intended and we are skilled, we can get disappointed. When we don't receive praise, we say that patients (or administrators, partners, friends, etc.) are ungrateful or that they have no idea what we go through to deliver quality care. *We can make ourselves and our satisfaction level dependent upon what we get in return* and that, my friends, is a form of victim mentality. Because we have a romanticized (and somewhat self-serving) expectation of outcome, we find our professional and relationship satisfaction levels declining. Does this mean we are hopeless in finding satisfaction in our chosen professions or relationships? Certainly not, but many have left medicine and relationships thinking so. I would suggest we are simply looking in the wrong place for satisfaction. It comes from within and the meanings we attach to all our experiences. So how do we get there?

Activating Our Resourcefulness

Resourceful (adj.) Ingenious, capable and full of initiative; using imagination in difficult situations, says the dictionary. Avoiding burnout or recovering from it requires an ability to be and remain resourceful. And remember, this is GOOD news because it means we have the potential to be in control of our internal state and the ability to tap into our own innate skill of being resourceful when we think we're stuck.

Marvin Minsky, a cognitive psychologist and scientist said in his book, *The Emotion Machine*: "So much of our human resourcefulness comes from having multiple ways to describe the same situations so that each one of those different perspectives may help us to get around the deficiencies of the other ones." This ability to dig into situations and view things in broad fashion is how we see possibility. Couple that with the ability to respond (instead of react) and choosing to mold ourselves differently at any given moment, makes us unstoppable. It's the adaptability that moves us forward.

As our self-awareness grows, so does our ability to consciously choose a different state or a different approach to what troubles us. It was again our friend Viktor Frankl who wisely said, "Between stimulus and response, there is a space. In that space is our power to choose our response. In our response lies our growth and our freedom." We can choose between serenity or fury. This is not to say that we serenely dismiss matters that need to be addressed, it means that we manage our emotions, our thoughts and our feelings in a way that has us coming from a resourceful place where we consider and choose a response best suited, rather than just reacting and using our small "critter brain" that operates on primitive survival instinct. It is this kind of resourcefulness and self-control that will get us to where we desire to be. Don't think for a minute that a successful outcome depends solely on the resources we have at our disposal. The ultimate outcome depends more on our resourcefulness to maximize what we've got.

How to activate resourcefulness is no big secret. It is in maximizing what we've got that we become "ingenious." It is when we integrate the concept of "My life is my own creation" that we become more capable because we see clearly the part we play in it and have taken off the shackles of victimness. The ideals of what we want to achieve become clearer and less dependent on circumstances. There's simply no room for burnout here, the excitement (and sometime even joy) of creating our reality dominates.

Burnout and its associated victimness is simply a wrong road taken. It's never too late to undo those shackles, change our route and forge a new perspective with our innate resourcefulness. If you think you're in burnout, try incorporating some of these practices, reading other motivational books, or get an education *in yourself* and develop personally. If you think others are in burnout, try sharing some of these ideas to ease their struggle. Truly, if Viktor Frankl could manage his mental state in a place as vile as Auschwitz, we can certainly manage in our modern world. We can change our life experience by working to change our perspective.

··· 13 ···

The Vitality Of Curiosity

"It is a miracle that curiosity survives a formal education."

Albert Einstein

THE GENIUSES WHO have walked among us exemplify the quality of curiosity. Excellence is rarely achieved without it. The reason is that when we are truly curious, we are not invested in a particular outcome. The British journalist Alistair Cooke put it this way: "Curiosity endows the people who have it with a generosity in argument and a serenity in their own mode of life which springs from their cheerful willingness to let life take the form it will." There is no shame attached to not having the answer or not understanding, there is instead an excitement to see how the story turns out.

Curiosity and a tolerance for uncertainty fosters learning and discovery. It liberates us to see ourselves as life-long learners. Fully embracing the fact that we will never have all the answers is actually somewhat of a relief! "Curiosity," says Cooke, "is free-wheeling intelligence" – a place where what we *do know* dances with *possibility*. It is the place where the rational and creative work together to find understanding with the delicious by-product of excitement in the discovery. Samuel Johnson, prolific writer and author of the English world's first substantial dictionary, recognized it this way: "Curiosity is one of the most permanent and certain characteristics of a vigorous intellect" and I couldn't agree more.

This brings us to what I have experienced as a downside to a curious intellect. Some do not have the patience for questions, others may feel threatened or perceive you as challenging the status quo. People often resist the prospect of change when we ask questions about why things are the way they are. This is rooted in the fixed mindset we discussed early on, where we are to reach a goal and finally be done and achieved a satis-factory endpoint. A growth mindset will always be reaching for more, and when we look at the most successful endeavors around us, we will discover that those involved usually live in a growth mindset. When encountering situations where there is resistance, there is some degree of skill and gentle nudging to get people on the side of curiosity. If you are going to take something on, the best advice I can offer is to first make the intent of your questions clear. Let others know that the earnest motivation for asking is for everyone's benefit. Also to pick your battles. Invest your efforts wisely with those you see potential in. You won't always be successful at getting others to entertain what you are curious about, but you will at least be modeling a positive behavior for continual improvement that others may consider later. We never know when the seed of curiosity will sprout!

Curiosity stokes the fire in our belly that drives us to con-stantly apply energy toward more knowledge and improved performance. One of the greatest gifts we can give is to join with another's curiosity and follow it to fruition. My father cul-tivated curiosity by answering my why questions not directly, but with a "Well, let's take a look and think about that." Using the spirit of curiosity, he would guide me through the process of what I did know and couple it with newly provided or self-dis-covered facts. I still remember the young-child thrill of watching my understanding unfold and grow. I still experience that excitement when I come across something new that sparks my interest. Having that habit of what I like to call "curiosity learning," gives us an exceptional ability to figure things out and adapt on the fly. Rather than fearing the unknowns, we can remain curious, adaptable and capable of incorporating our new discoveries.

Everyone, no matter what role we're in, can nurture curiosity. When we carry the mentality of curiosity, we create environments that are energized by the pursuit of greater knowledge. Because the focus is on growth, we naturally avoid assigning shame to not knowing. There is a pervasive excitement because we anticipate that something new will be learned. We can live quite a dull life without it!

Teamwork can thrive in this environment as we learn to respect the knowledge of others and the exploration of unknowns becomes less scary. We watch the knowledgeable come up against what they don't know. We are encouraged when they model curiosity and look for greater understanding. It is through this process that we come to accept that it's okay not to have all the answers. We experience the spirit-renewing thrill of learning and discovery. Excellence in practice thrives here.

Curiosity can also enliven relationships. We often have a habit of drawing conclusions based on very little fact when it comes to others. We can hesitate to ask clarifying questions to avoid the downsides I mentioned about curiosity. We even make stuff up to explain another's actions rather than risk misinterpretation. Being curious and asking questions to clarify a person's viewpoint or intent goes a long way to improve communication, and far more often has positive results than negative. Our worldview expands with these newly discovered perspectives; even our compassion and empathy for others will find fertile soil to grow when we apply a little curiosity.

Curiosity is a generator of vitality. It adds richness and excitement to all that we do and life is never boring when we practice it. Be curious, ask the questions you wonder about— the answers can often be surprising, fascinating, and even delightful. I have no doubt you will be exhilarated by the practice and I'm certain you will smile and laugh more than you expect. Become a curious person and your love of the job, your team and your life will grow.

··· 14 ···

Balancing Our Life Experiences Through Mindfulness

"Mindfulness is simply being aware of what is happening right now without wishing it were different. Enjoying the pleasant without holding on when it changes (which it will). Being with the unpleasant without fearing it will always be this way (which it won't)."

James Baraz

OUR ABILITY TO remain resourceful hinges largely on a well-balanced life. Being balanced hinges largely on being mindful. This is so important that I felt the topic of mindful living deserves its own chapter. Research has demonstrated that the application of mindfulness has clear benefits to enhances our life experience overall.

How do we know if we are mindful? Our lives will speak to that question. Our degrees of joy, ease, wellness and satisfaction are all barometers of how mindful we are. Mindfulness is a practice I tune up and redeploy to recover balance when I feel ill at ease and am seeking answers. It is the primary habit I attribute to my increasing happiness over the years. It's about being fully present, taking in all of what the moment offers. Living mindfully provides clearer perspective, enhances our depth of experience, and can provide the necessary pause and relief from life's pressures.

In medicine we see heart-wrenching things that bring us face-to-face with the universal fear of vulnerability and death. Managing our reaction to such stressors takes mindfulness so they don't wring us dry emotionally, physically and spiritually, or turn us into disconnected, unfeeling creatures. As mentioned in our discussions of balance and burnout, having other aspects of our lives which replenish our inner stores is part of a satisfying life. We need activities that let us experience joy and gratitude for the simple goodness of life. Doing these activities mindfully gives them greater strength. Even short amounts of time doing so can go a long way because they provide a respite of sorts from the pressures of life. Take for example a practice I use to maintain balance while I am working. During my half-hour lunch break I escape to nature on the hospital grounds. Even if it is inclement weather I make a point to step outside or sit by a window and take in some fresh air, look at the beauty of the snow, rain or glorious sunshine and consciously experience peace inside me. I avoid my phone and other distractions so that I can stop the chatter in my head and rest awhile in my heart. I try not to let things like texting or email interrupt me, and this break allows me to connect with the solid foundation of who I am and keeps me from feeling like life is running me over.

As I am writing this portion of the book, I am sitting in an old stone cottage on the Pacific Ocean. It is a bright sunny day, but the wind is howling. I can see it whipping the brush on the dunes and making whitecaps for miles out over the water. Even the people walking on the path have to lean forward into the wind, their hair whipping about their heads. The birds brave enough to be airborne do not flap their wings as the force of the wind keeps them aloft. At the same time, I am sitting warm and dry in my rock house, basking in the sun shining through the windows while the outside world is being buffeted about. This is a great metaphor for how I feel when I take the time to create balance as I do on my lunch break. This stone cottage and ocean story is a worthy visualization exercise to help re-center, allowing the winds of life to be whirling while we sit comfortably in the stone house of our minds and hearts, complete with sunshine coming through the windows.

This mindfulness principle was certainly put to the test when it came to the COVID-19 events. Being restricted from so many things I enjoyed, I had to just be present and enjoy life in a simpler way. Brooding over what I missed would not serve me, but enjoying what I did have kept me strong and resilient. I learned much about what was really important to me and created happiness in my world, with a realization about how valuable a simplified life is. My appreciation for nature was deepened during this time which I would not have guessed was possible given the depth of my love for it. I derived an incredible amount of enjoyment watching elements of nature around me which I believe spared me from the angst that many experienced given what was in the news during that time.

Your own rituals for balance are likely to exist already, even if you don't regularly or consciously do them. Don't make the mistake of saving mindfulness for your relaxing vacations. Make time for these rituals and be fully present and mindful when doing them. If we allow distracting thoughts, cell-phone activities, mindless distractions or worries take over those activities, we effectively drown out their rejuvenating aspects. Say, for instance, that taking a daily walk is your ritual. Allowing thoughts to be preoccupied with troubles or letting your phone intrude on this sacred time can reduce its full benefits, which was likely intended to unwind, release tension and re-energize.

I read an article in *Time Magazine* some years ago about the growing numbers of people joining the Mindfulness-Based Stress Reduction (MBSR) technique developed by Jon Kabat-Zinn, an

MIT-educated scientist. Kabat-Zinn explains mindfulness this way:

> "It's the awareness that arises through paying attention, on purpose, in the present moment and non-judgmentally. That sounds pretty simple...but actually when we start paying attention to how much we pay attention, half of the time our minds are all over the place and we have a very hard time sustaining attention."

Learning mindfulness can be achieved through the incorporation of certain activities that begin to train our minds to focus. Walking with mindful attention to all that is around us, sitting quietly and paying attention to our breathing, creative endeavors, pausing for a moment to watch a bird search for breakfast in the lawn, doing something not done before, unitasking, not answering the cell phone each time it rings and taking time to just let your mind wander, where the mindfulness practice is to just observe where it goes. These are some of things that practitioners of being mindful regularly engage in.

There are nearly 1,000 certified instructors teaching MBSR in more than thirty countries. The military is using the technique for combat veterans to help get them back on track with their lives. Major corporations are offering classes to their employees and some even offer on-site quiet space for meditation, an ancient main-stay practice where we can learn to focus and be more mindful.

Learning mindfulness has widespread application. With its practice, the research shows we can rewire our brains to achieve a less-stressed state, which enhances our physical health. These practices have been shown to lower cortisol levels, reduce blood pressure, manage chronic pain, boost immunity and possibly even impact the kind of gene expression that morphs its way into diseases like cancer. So enticing are the discoveries that investment in mindfulness practices exploded in 2006 and millions of grant money began to be awarded to study the effects of

mindfulness in greater depth. In 2021, PubMed Central identified 16,581 publications since the year 1966, with 68% occurring
in the psychology and psychiatric scientific journals noting its
effectiveness.

All mindfulness practices have in common the simple direc-
tive to be fully present in the moment—tasting the raisin in your
mouth, feeling its texture; walking, noticing the way your heel
hits the ground first, the smell of damp soil underfoot and the
sunshine through the trees; mindfully sitting quietly noticing the
interruptive thoughts and going with the flow of them, noticing
how they change as you reach greater calm; or a concentration
type of meditation where you deliberately dismiss thoughts and
refocus on the concentration technique. By incorporating mindful practices in our high-stress lives, we give the brain a break to
focus and function in greater calm.

A reduced ability to be mindful has also been noted to have
detrimental effects on our brain function. This declining ability
is believed to be rooted in our near-constant connectivity with
technology and the incessant stimuli being registered in our
brains. Its constant barrage distracts us from being fully present with whatever the current moment holds. We now know
that our brains have what is called neuroplasticity, where they
become altered by whatever is they are routinely exposed to.
In our highly interruptive world, research is showing that multitasking is leading to an overall reduction in productivity. Even
high-level executives with the comfortable corner office and
control of their schedules are reporting this. This reduced productivity has a compounding effect on the level of stress we
experience.

It is in the training of mindfulness that we begin to get the
brain back to practicing fully focused attention. As we do so, it—
like a muscle—gets stronger and its ability to readily access that
fully focused state becomes greater. With mindfulness, sorting
through our priorities becomes simpler and our stress is reduced
because we are attending to what matters most, not what is
screaming loudest. Mindfulness also allows us to unwind when

we have a spare moment, such as when we take a deep breath of fresh air or listen to the symphony of sounds as we walk to our next meeting. Mindfulness gives us the refreshing break from it all that we need to keep the stressors of life managed.

Mindfulness also entails learning to see how things are inter-connected, how they are responsive to and influenced by each other. Awareness of all we are experiencing in a given moment will begin to draw back the curtain to a higher level of clarity and cognizance where the context of the moment is more completely comprehended. Mindfulness enhances our skills as an observer of others and our own thoughts, generating more finely tuned responses to situations. Without mindfulness we *react* at a more instinctual gut level, which is more driven by survival instinct—a survival instinct seldom necessary in the modern world.

Contextually aware responses, on the other hand, are enlightened by this greater comprehension and are guided more by values and desired end-points, rather than mere survival. Problems are more brilliantly solved with this level of aware-ness because our comprehension of all factors is greater. In that enlightened, responsive state, we are also more apt to experi-ence the satisfaction of having contributed our absolute best. Maintaining a broad awareness makes us far more apt to leave a legacy that we can reflect on with satisfaction and pride because we have exercised our fullest potential and know that we made a difference where we could. It is this kind of conscious living that offers the greatest possibility of excellence and where we can live in the sweet-spot.

It's worth rementioning here that worry and regret are two of the most ineffective and distracting states that can derail mind-fulness. Worry occupies us with the future, which is subject to change, and regret occupies us with the past, which cannot be undone. Such preoccupation distracts us from whatever oppor-tunities the current moment holds and can color them unfairly by association with the *what was* or *what might be* instead of seeing *what is*. This does not mean we don't prepare for the future or neglect cleaning up the messes we have made in the past, but allowing them to persistently distract us does not serve us. Perhaps the most wonderful thing of all is, the more mindful we become, the less worry and regret we experience because we have taken the best of care to manage our moments. Our messes are fewer, life is easier and our confidence grows to handle whatever the future brings.

Learning to be mindful and fully present in the moment not only maximizes our effectiveness, it also gives us the ability to drink in simple, unadulterated joy when it presents itself. This is where we will find the lifeblood that sustains who we are. Taking the moment to really listen and connect with a patient or a friend, hear their stories and concerns, and offer them comfort feeds our human need to belong. If we are only partially present with others, preoccupied with those past concerns or what task we have to do next, we completely miss out on the sustenance current circumstances offer us. It is the loss of this full engagement that creates our sense of disconnection and perhaps feeling we don't belong.

All we have at any given time is the present moment. Our ability to mindfully manage the moment, being thoughtfully responsive and embracing whatever it holds, is the smartest and most prosperous investment we can make in our futures. Mindfulness makes us 100% "in," with all our talents and abilities to apply toward success and creates the brightest possible futures. Mindfulness nurtures us, providing the room to pause, drink in and be refreshed by the simple wonders of life, wherever we happen to find them. I hope I have inspired you to start looking, I suspect you'll notice even more wonders than expected.

···15···

Fulfillment, Being Enough And The Inside-Out Nature Of Things

"If you live for the approval of others, you will die by their rejection."

Pastor Rick Warren

SO BY NOW you get the idea that being fulfilled by life is mostly an inside job. Our internal environment has the greatest influence in determining our satisfaction, but often we get lost in looking for it outside of ourselves. When we don't get what we seek, we feel disappointed and doubt our abilities and success as a whole. As a remedy to this, I want to explore what I like to call the inside-out nature of things.

Most of us are not in the habit of taking stock of what we do well. We are more likely to focus on what needs to be improved. It is a habit that we impose upon ourselves and that others impose on us. While this is well intended and improving is necessary for forward movement, our own self-generated appreciation for what has been accomplished is an equally important part of the equation. Like many things in life, we can't utterly neglect one side of a thing without paying a price. So let's dig a little deeper into this inside-out thing.

If we require and are dependent on an outside source of validation, we can wait a long time! We can worry if we are enough and will sometimes even wait until an external acknowledgement arrives before we believe that we have done well and are deserving of praise. This lopsided preoccupation on our flaws and our need for external approval can have us slowly withering and dying because we are overly dependent on the outside world to feed us. To really enjoy life, we must celebrate our progress regularly and intentionally, generating acknowledgement *from the inside-out*.

The impact of our efforts as nurses or as other healthcare providers is enormous. I did not fully appreciate just how true this is until I became a patient myself on the receiving end of care. Our words, tone, patience, ability to explain things and expertise have a huge impact on a patient's experience and overall outcome. Yet, we seem to dismiss these good works as "just part of the job" and fail to appreciate how deeply we do impact those around us by our words, deeds and thoughts. Failing to appreciate this may also have us miss opportunities for even greater impact. There is even a bias toward NOT praising our efforts because that would be overstating things; after all, it is the expected standard of the job to do what we do. Because of our idealized professional standards and lopsided focus on continual improvement, we can find ourselves feeling like we're never quite enough. Our awareness of fault can become so dominant that we become blind to success.

In my view, internal acknowledgement of good work only becomes a negative and overstated if we are boastful with the implication that we are somehow better than others. If we are truly an individual that is always striving for better, part of the inside job is to build our own self-awareness of where we succeed and nurture ourselves with those successes. The job, and life for that matter, are just too hard without this.

For my own sanity I typically use the ride home to take stock of how things went. When things don't go well I think about what I can learn from the experience; then create a plan to do better next time. Following this, I recall the things that did go well...and celebrate them! I take stock of how I've improved or succeeded and allow feelings of gratitude to fill me up.

At home we practice this too. My husband and I have a habit on the weekends, after a hard day's work on a project, of conducting an "admiration phase." This usually involves a refreshing beverage and a stroll around the project to admire it. We may talk a bit on how we pulled it off, the obstacles we overcame, what we love most about it, whatever applies, and we make a toast. A friend of mine taught me this and we love it! This habit saved our sanity when we were undergoing an extensive remodel of our home that was seemingly never-ending. It's how we got through all the challenges we encountered. Gratitude is a force multiplier of happiness and should never be underestimated.

No matter how small the win might be, take the time to acknowledge good work. Allow yourself a congratulatory smile or an out loud "WHOO-HOO!!!!" for those really big wins. Savoring success is not inappropriately self-serving, you are just respecting and celebrating the life you've invested in. You're no victim-wallflower in life...you are the starring quarterback, calling the plays that get you to your goals. As we live this way, the need for external validation diminishes. Internal satisfaction rises with the recognition of our good works. Acknowledging this congruence with our goals and core values gives us peace.

This kind of recognition and support holds true for our coworkers as well. Validation and celebration of others can be a powerful experience in team building. Talk with others, ask them how their day went, support them in their challenges and compliment them on a job well done. Encourage them when they miss the mark or feel discouraged. This simple act of kindness can inspire inside-out living for them as well.

I remember a time in my life where I found it hard to compliment others. It somehow felt that when I did, I was acknowledging them as better than me, which was because I had the perspective that outward validation is what defined my success. I set about promising myself I would find places to acknowledge the good work of others and it enhanced my relationships with colleagues tremendously. This kind of mutual celebration promotes a cohesive team and fosters excitement and satisfaction. It makes the bar visible and continues to raise it for the team. It helps people integrate their successes at an internal level and how their interdependence on one another created something greater than what they can accomplish alone. Team excellence is born from this type of synergy. Giving to others in this way energizes the group because the team will feel rewarded, unified in the good work they do, and together wanting to excel even more.

Being Enough

As it turns out, most of us struggle with doubts about being enough, wondering if we are valued and if we are acceptable given our imperfections. Both in relationships and in the pursuit of professional accomplishments, being mired in this can even make failure more likely. Those doubts can result in behaviors that do not bring us more of what we want. For example, doubt can be masked as brazen arrogance, where the fear of not being enough is aggressive, where we posture and try to exaggerate who we really are. That never goes well. The opposite response to doubt is to be passive, that person who never risks and feels unfulfilled because of it.

The fear of not being enough is pervasive enough in our society that those who study such things have even given it names: "the Impostor Syndrome," "Imposter Phenomenon" or "Fraud Syndrome." It is a recognized psychological condition in which people are unable to internalize their own accomplishments. Despite external evidence of competence, these people remain convinced, worried or concerned with varying degrees

Finding Your Sweet-Spot in the World of Healthcare

of intensity, that they are frauds and do not deserve the success they have achieved. They dismiss proof of success as luck, timing, or as a result of deceiving others into thinking they are more intelligent and competent than they believe themselves to be.

Interestingly, it is a malady more prominent in highly educated and successful people, being more prevalent in women than in men. The syndrome is about the person's source of anxiety being wrapped around a fear of being "discovered" or "found out" for their weaknesses. It's a worry that someone will discover they don't have all the answers and are not as smart as others think they are. This way of being exists, hidden and unknown to others, in some brilliant people. I can't help but wonder if it exists, at least in part, from our need to over-validate our children, even if they did nothing special. It is not a big stretch to appreciate that if "everyone gets a trophy" it could leave a child's immature mind a bit confused about what accomplishment is. Teaching them to self-appreciate will serve them so much better when they grow up and adjust to the adult world where trophies are fewer and further between.

Many of us, if not most of us, occasionally find ourselves doubting our abilities and fretting about not measuring up. We worry about how we will, or if we will, connect the dots that give us the answers or if we will have clarity about what to do next. Research clearly demonstrates that the brain in states of worry like this can short-circuit our abilities to draw on our strengths and makes us less able to problem-solve. Worry, in and of itself, is a state that can make us stuck and can create the very state we fear—that of being frozen and unable to move forward.

Our thoughts are powerful. Never underestimate their ability to help or hamper your life and your goals. What we think about, how we view things, always has an effect on how we show up in life. There's a balance between integrating both the wins and the learning opportunities. By equally promoting both we begin to be more satisfied with our progress and are better able to embrace every part of who we are, warts and all.

149

Sitting on Pins and Needles

Being mindful of the inside-out nature of things can also serve us well when dealing with the uncertainties of human interaction. Have you ever had the experience when working with others, or when in relationship with particular individuals, where you feel edgy, uneasy and worrying about every little thing you say and do because of the response you might get? Maybe they seem to be reactive, overly sensitive or are somehow consistently trying to demonstrate how they are superior. Perhaps you avoid wearing your "Best mom in the world" embroidered scrubs your children gave you because you know your coworker has a poor relationship with their own children. Maybe you avoid talking about how excited you are about singing with a band next Friday night because you worry others would view it as bragging. Or maybe, at the expense of the patient, you do not gently offer your knowledge because you're concerned about embarrassing your coworker.

Environments or relationships that demonstrate traits such as these are weak in their character. Often they have the hallmark of being harshly judgmental, which in turn breeds competitiveness to quell the angst created when living in such an environment. Many do see this for what it is, are repelled by it, and either rail against it, leave it or quietly live in intimidation. During the course of my career I have witnessed these kinds of environments and it saddens me greatly. One thing for sure, my nature is incapable of living in quiet intimidation. I have asked myself many times, "How can such bright people be so wholly unaware of this culture's toxicity?" I think it is our lack of awareness for the price we pay for such behaviors that have us continuing to do them. If left unchecked or unaddressed, these dynamics normalize. I've even heard such casual remarks as, "Oh that's just how Sean is, he picks on every new person," like being a bully is on par with conversations about the weather.

Having a private conversation with a berating physician or a coworker we are in conflict with may seem like the last thing we want to do, but the vulnerable populations we care for depend on our professionalism to do so. Taking this risk has cost me at times, but I do not regret having taken a stand. Emotional dominance and inappropriate subordination of others grows by our acquiescence to it. This is precisely the environment where gang mentality, cliques, gossip and various forms of bullying take root. All become distractors from delivering excellent care. When we "go along to get along" with such behaviors, we'll never achieve the kind of harmonious, exceptional workplaces we all dream of. More likely we'll perpetuate cyclical conflict, dysfunction and more serious acts of bullying or sabotage, even violence. We can watch talent walk right out the door because of it, causing organizations to flush all the wages, hours and efforts invested to select and train a person right down the toilet. So clearly, sitting on pins and needles with others places us in a severely handicapped position when it comes to fiscal responsibility, team cooperation, collaboration, creativity, and ultimately excellence in patient care. The rippling effects cost organizations millions, the costs to patients can only be guessed at. How can we in good conscience idly tolerate it?

It was a very sage advisor of mine who wisely said, "Ninety-five percent of the time how people act has nothing to do with you." All of us have demons to conquer, so it behooves us—if we want to be effective change agents in our environments—to remember that and not take such behaviors personally when we are dealing with others who are behaving badly or attempting to exert some degree of emotional dominance. Something I have come to understand is this; most people behave badly because they are fearful to some degree of being enough, that very human worry that's created when we compare ourselves to the outside world and have yet to learn how to effectively mentor and appreciate ourselves. It's helpful to remember this when strategizing and executing actions to rectify our relationships. I'm not suggesting we become anyone's therapist, but remembering that many behaviors come from feelings of inferiority and worry about being enough, can give us the objectivity that avoids an ineffective, emotional-based response. Compassionate kindness can go a long way towards creating cultures of trust, acceptance and safety.

Many well intentioned leaders believe they are doing well and serving their teams by lending an ear and validating the feelings of every voiced concern. While listening is important, often such attempts do not steer towards a resolution and can lack respect toward the accused. Most interpersonal complaints are rooted in nothing more than differences in personality or in style rather than any breach of responsibility. Long-term management of this type usually ends up with the loudest complainers and bullies forming the culture and opinions, having been inspired by the seeming justification given by the well-intentioned leader. Ostracization and alienation occurs and if your organization has an unfavorable turnover rate, this lack of tolerance for others is often the source. "The tail wags the dog" or "The inmates run the asylum" are phrases that describe this end result.

The job of leadership is to create unity and help teams understand that varying styles and personalities can be appreciated and worked with. It broadens our perspectives to have this variety. Coaching teams to see conflicts rooted in personality or style for what they are, rather than right or wrong positions, moves teams to refocus on their purpose and the job at hand. As leaders, when an employee brings a complaint to us, it is important to emphasize that we want everyone to be successful. Too often we do not offer this in conversation and forget that we are hearing one side of the story. Everyone deserves a fair shake and it serves us to remember that most often it takes two to tango when it comes to conflict. All parties must take ownership for their part in the disruption. Most often this can be achieved by sitting down with all involved, facilitating the conversation so that it remains respectful and goal directed. It may sound time consuming, but do this consistently and people will get the message the expectation is they problem solve without you, like mature adults, rather than gossip about or try to destroy another's reputation. They will be more developed and effective as a team for having done so.

Honestly, most of our differences don't amount to a hill of beans when it's all said and done. Why not allow others to be themselves? If there is no serious concern of harm to others or dereliction of duty, why the need to gossip, discredit or back-bite? Conversely, I also see too much focus on *how* we are diverse making it more important than the job at hand, which only make resentments grow towards differences. We are better served to focused on gifts, talents and abilities that each bring to the table. Just because someone doesn't seem to fit in doesn't mean they don't have things to offer that better the team. After all, there is the expectation in the workplace that we are professional colleagues, not "besties." We often cheat ourselves out of learning and growth when we exclude others because we hold too tightly to this belief that people need to fit in.

Sitting back, judging and excluding gives us the illusion of feeling safe, but it really just keeps our worlds small and limited in possibility. As leaders, whether we hold the formal title or not, we can encourage others to be open, accepting and charitable. We become stronger being multi-faceted, capable of much more because we have a greater group of varied talent and perspective at the table. Differing opinions and ways of approaching things often have too much stock placed in them. Often such battles are fought over things of little consequence. Our relationships with others are far more important than winning or proving ourselves right.

Susan M. Heathfield, a highly respected management consultant, notes that if managers are in the habit of giving private audience to employees to hear out grievances regarding another individual, they become entangled in the conflict. This is a well-researched and documented dynamic called Triangulation. The employee complaining will present their own biased report, because they have a vested interest in proving themselves right, and will frame themselves as the Victim of the other employee who is the Persecutor. Through this private audience the manager, perhaps without even realizing it, is effectively placed in the position of Rescuer. Though the offered listening and empathy is well intended, allowing it without mentoring the parties *jointly* to solve their workplace problems in an effective way only perpetuates polarization and defensiveness. This can even spread to the rest of the team as worry about being talked about spreads, and others begin to engage in Triangulation. This scenario happens in all sorts of business and personal relationships. The dynamic of operating from these three positions is never-ending. The cycle repeats over and over again, with people moving between these roles. I have worked in units that are mired in this kind of dysfunction. It takes one person, usually the manager, to step outside the triangulation and not engage in rescuing. The victim and persecutor can also disengage by saying, "Let's work this out together."

A manager bears responsibility for setting communication guidelines and the expectation that adult-to-adult resolution be reached. While this effort is time consuming, it is an investment in the team's future effectiveness and employee retention. It is a manager's job to get work done through the teams they manage. Get the parties face to face! In this meeting the manager can mediate and guide the conversation in accordance with the organization's goals and purposes, while assuring respectful dialog, goal setting, change and progress.

Ms. Heathfield outlines the following approach:

- Meet with the antagonists together. Let each briefly summarize their point of view, without comment or interruption by the other party. This should be a short discussion so that all parties are clear about the disagreement and conflicting views. Intervene if either employee attacks the other employee. This is not acceptable.

- Ask each participant to describe specific actions they'd like to see the other party take that would resolve the differences. Three or four suggestions work well. An example is, "I'd like

Mary to send the report to me by Thursday at 1:00 PM so I can complete my assignment by my due date of Friday at noon."

- Sometimes, you as the supervisor, must own some of the responsibility for helping the employees resolve their conflict. Always ask, "What about the work situation is causing these staff members to fail?"

- If the situation needs further exploration, use a process adapted from Stephen Covey in which you ask each participant to additionally identify what the other employee can do more of, less of, stop and start.

- All participants discuss and commit to making the changes necessary to resolve the conflict. Commit to noticing that the other person has made a change, no matter how small. Commit to treating each other with dignity and respect. It is okay to have reasonable disagreements over issues and plans; it is never okay to have personality conflicts that affect the workplace.

- Let the antagonists know that you will not choose sides. It is impossible for a person external to the conflict to know the truth of the matter. You expect the individuals to resolve the conflicts proactively as adults. If they are unwilling to do so, you will be forced to take disciplinary action that can lead to dismissal for both parties.

- Finally, assure both parties that you have every faith in their ability to resolve their differences and get on with their successful contributions within your shared organization. Set a time to review progress.

Ideally, the face to face approach can cultivate a comfort level where these complaints or unmet needs can be addressed in adult-to-adult constructive ways. Often it comes down to correcting misunderstanding and perceptions. And don't confuse this with a therapy session though referring someone to an Employee Assistance Program for this may be appropriate. This is a business meeting to uncover the barriers to working as a team. Genuine expression of desired success of both parties is imperative. The manager's ultimate goal being to give the permission and tools for people to handle conflict effectively on their own, coupled with the expectation for a mutually agreeable, win-win outcome, not win-lose. With this approach, the coworkers are given the expectation that they are to *invest in and help create each other's success,* a principle that has been called "managing up" coworkers. They will learn that running to the boss to tattle-tail is not a route supported and that the bottom line is that behaviors interfering with the work to be done are not tolerated.

Our long-standing habits can stand in the way of how we think about others, our circumstances and ourselves. Learning to be self-aware, noticing habits of fear, and grasping the handicapping effect, more easily happens when managers foster a team culture where all can feel accepted for human vulnerabilities while being supported to bravely master them. We can model this by sharing our own stories of discovery, which can grow team confidence in doing their own internal work and all members begin to appreciate that making mistakes and missing the mark at times is part of life, not a definition of self or a lasting point of shame. If all parties are transparent and open about concerns and challenges to overcome, we can demonstrate that struggle and worry are common experiences, and that it is possible to manage and not be consumed by them. Dealing kindly and compassionately with unwanted behavior may relax defensiveness enough for people to become aware of the causes, giving them a leverage point to work on what needs to be changed.

Viewing others from the inside-out means we take a moment to consider that all of us, at least on occasion, exhibit weaknesses that produce poor choices in how we show up in life. Rather than pronouncing a person defective in some way, take a minute to consider that the behavior you are seeing isn't likely their best self. Be kind and patient and you may be just the right catalyst to make a big difference. I remember a nursing school instructor who once pulled me into a storeroom and spoke kindly and compassionately about a irritable attitude I was displaying. Unbeknownst to her, I was going through a long-term relationship breakup and the failure of this relationship had me greatly doubting my self-worth. Her genuine kindness was powerful. I burst into tears when I realized she was making this effort because she understood what she was seeing was not my best, but perhaps related to things occurring on the inside. We talked only for a few minutes, but I was uplifted, encouraged and left with a new perspective. That was more than thirty-five years ago yet I remember it, and her, with vivid detail. It was a catalyst for change and the beginning of my understanding that whatever we hold inside, inevitably manifests outside.

"Over-Packing The Cannon"

If we put too much gunpowder in a cannon, it will make a lot of noise but the ball will overshoot the target and fail in its purpose. Likewise, self-doubt can show up in the habit of overstating circumstances. (You know, the drama queens/kings.) It was a long-standing tendency of mine to present concerns in big and dramatic ways as a means for me to overcome my fear of not being understood or heard. While I've made large strides in managing this, I still sometime see that tendency when I am less than centered or confident.

I've noticed that I'm not alone in this. Over-dramatization is something quite prevalent in healthcare arenas. I believe it exists because we don't have confidence that simple, rational truth is enough. As nurses, perhaps this is because we have historically been secondary members of the team and have not always been valued for our observations. We have evolved from an ancillary staff position of changing bedpans and bandages to highly skilled professionals, but the cultures in some places have not caught up. Physicians, by contrast, are less likely to overstate circumstances because they have a long-standing culture of authoritative certainty. If we don't feel valued for our opinion as a professional part of the team, we may believe we have to be dramatic and loud to be heard.

The predictable result of overstating and dramatizing circumstances is that people stop listening because it is difficult to hear an exaggerated statement. Overstating and dramatizing reduces credibility and can sound more hysterical than rational. Many listeners have the tendency to disregard it entirely rather than take the time to sift through it and get to the root of the concern. It is in remembering inside-out philosophy that helps us sort through this type of distortion, both when we listen to others or when we want to express ourselves clearly without the drama. As we begin to understand our fears and manage them, our courage grows to present our best selves and articulately state our concerns.

Let's help each other in the quest of being the best we are capable of. If you notice someone being overly critical of themselves or feeling defeated, remind them of the good they have achieved. If others are being dramatic, assure them that you can and want to hear them. No one should feel a need to over-pack the cannon to get a point across.

Everyone has a part in creating environments where effective communication is alive and well. We all have our inside-out stuff. We become more patient when we remember that people have a life hidden from our view that influences our interactions. Don't take things so personally, cut people a little slack sometimes, and above all, do your own work so your inside-out is genuine, kind and constructive—both to others and yourself.

··· 16 ···

Individual Leadership

"The challenge of leadership is to be strong, but not rude; be kind, but not weak; be bold, but not bully; be thoughtful, but not lazy; be humble, but not timid; be proud, but not arrogant; have humor, but without folly."

Jim Rohn

DEMONSTRATING INDIVIDUAL LEADERSHIP is really the life-long endeavor of becoming our best selves and leading by example in the world, whether we hold a position of formal authority or not. Leadership is inescapable. We are at very least leaders of our own development. We unavoidably demonstrate by example in the world, so there is a decision to be made: what kind of leader we will be? Like it or not, consciously or unconsciously, we provide leadership no matter where we are or what we are doing. Our demonstrations of integrity, patience, generosity and kindness—either lacking or in abundance—effectively lead others to do the same.

Too often we ascribe the responsibility of leadership to those administratively or formally superior to ourselves. This is a habit of work life, but can also be victim-oriented thinking if we want to be without responsibility and don't see our part in creating what is. It gets us off the hook from acknowledging our behaviors have impact—for better or for worse. We also tend to ascribe outcomes and circumstances as the sole doing of those in charge as well, blaming or attributing to them both failure and success, as though they were the only ones with influence. While no one can argue those who carry a bigger stick have positions of leverage, the fact still remains we have the ability to effect change no matter where we are in the structure of things.

We effect change all the time. Trouble is, we fail to recognize we are having influence, good or bad, by our action or inaction. Our kind act may be the one thing that results in another act of kindness, because as people experience being cared about, they in turn often become more caring. The opposite is also very true. History and stories of human existence down through the ages give abundant evidence to how one small act or failure to act changed the course of world events.

Practicing individual leadership means we lead from within whatever circle of influence we live in. Consider the so-called "stars" of reality shows in today's media. It is unfortunate many have become enamored with them because their influence has not been entirely healthy. Badly behaving people lead by example. Millions of viewers subconsciously register outrageous and often times immoral, crude, unkind and deceitful behaviors as somehow not as bad as we thought, because the "star" is doing them! They must be somewhat acceptable or they would not be making thousands of dollars off this show, right?

Watching such things have consequences too; the most common being that our distrust of one another grows, followed by a loosening of the reins on our own inappropriate impulses and behaviors. If we want to be leaders striving toward a purposeful and noble life, we must surround ourselves and study the examples of those who are purposeful and noble. If we want to be excellent in what we do, we have to study those who are excellent. It behooves us to shut out the noise of those who pick a less purposeful existence.

Our ability to lead by example grows as we evolve, and no matter what age or experience, there is always opportunity to do so. Are we not inspired by the sweetness one child may show another? The greeting-card companies are making a fortune on that premise. You may be a brand-new nurse who is still "wet behind the ears," but there's opportunity to lead by example when you display compassion for patients, are respectful in your communication, are humble and willing to learn. This can inspire your seniors because it may remind them of some things they perhaps have lost sight of.

Reflecting on how we are informally leading in the world is necessary if we are earnest about living consciously, living fully and creating our own happiness. If we are seasoned professionals, how are we leading as the experienced practitioner? Are we patient with those learning? Are we kind to our team members? Do we practice compassion? Can we say that we lead our community by demonstrating awareness of good health through the example of maintaining our own health? If we choose not to display our best selves, we will harbor our own disappointment in our choices and experience a gnawing unhappiness.

It is a courageous act to honestly evaluate our own behaviors and lead ourselves into being better. Adjusting where needed brings confidence and strength. As we grow toward the person we want to be, our own sense of meaning, purpose and influence expands. Others are likely to notice our ability to lead—formally or informally—and the difference we are making in the world. Our circle of influence grows, one small act at a time. This is how the positive changes we hope for gain momentum.

$\bullet \bullet \bullet$ 17 $\bullet \bullet \bullet$

The Power Of True Connection

"Self-absorption in all its forms kills empathy, let alone compassion. When we focus on ourselves, our world contracts as our problems and preoccupations loom large. But when we focus on others, our world expands. Our own problems drift to the periphery of the mind and so seem smaller and we increase our capacity for connection—or compassionate action."

Daniel Goleman, author of *Emotional Intelligence*

IT WAS A quiet Sunday morning when I arrived for work in the Emergency Department. I loved working Sundays for a lot of reasons; one being the lack of traffic I have to endure and the other being that Sundays always have a special quietness. The lack of administrative personnel creates a more relaxed atmosphere and the old traditions of spiritual pursuit and family still seem to mark it as a special day of the week.

I sat down to receive report on my patients. One of them was a young man in his late twenties whom I'll call Michael. When the nurse began her report on him, she lowered her voice to a whisper saying, "He's here for homicidal ideation," a term we use when patients have thoughts of killing others. "He's been

here for four days and we are still waiting for an admission bed."
I asked about his demeanor and she reported he had been cooperative, didn't talk much and she was not aware of any aggression while in our care. She did not know many more details than that, only that the psychiatrist had started a new medication. I went to assess my other patients and then sat down to read Michael's chart before introducing myself to him.

As I read through the psychiatry report my heart ached. Michael was a military man who had PTSD. The primary origin of it was during his assignment as a prison guard at Guantanamo Bay where some of the worst-of-the-worst Islamist terrorists were held. As a guard, he was instructed not to interact with the detainees and specifically ordered not to react when the prisoners threw feces and urine at him or verbally assaulted him. He bravely endured months of this and returned home a reactionary and angry man.

He reported to the psychiatry team that his homicidal fixation was toward Muslims and for his superiors and governmental agencies who had not protected him. He could not reconcile the abuse he endured or understand why those in authority allowed it to occur, and he obsessively thought about the injustice. Not surprisingly, he also found himself getting in fights and disproportionately seething with anger in response to relatively minor events he perceived as disrespectful. He came to our ED because he knew if he didn't get a handle on it, he would eventually end up hurting someone or in jail. He had tried to navigate the VA system, but had been unable to make progress.

I got up and knocked on his door. "May I come in?" He nodded yes. His eyes were dull and furtive. He seemed hesitant to trust or perhaps embarrassed that a young, fit man of his age was lying in a hospital bed. I came in and sat down on a chair. "Hi Michael, I'm CJ, your nurse for the day. I have reviewed your chart, but first want to say how grateful I am for your service to this country. I don't take my freedom lightly and I know much of what I enjoy is due to the protection of brave men like you." Ah, there he was...the man inside...a momentary shine in the eye, a quick glance in my direction as though to assess my sincerity. I continued, "I also want to say how sorry I am you had to endure those horrific experiences at the prison, no one should have to bear that." There it was again...a glimmer of connection the eyes reveal as he now stared into mine. "Thank you," he said simply. Human-to-human connection had happened and we began to talk. Much of it standard evaluation questions one would expect a nurse to ask during a psychiatric assessment, and some about what he hoped to turn around in his life. I shared a few of my own experiences when his renditions had something in common with mine, and I shared what I found helpful to move me forward. I told him I made plenty of mistakes and decided to learn from them rather than be defeated. When he said "I feel almost jealous that you are where you are." I shared how hard I had to work at making my life what I wanted—and continue to work at it—and how I had to consciously decide I would not allow my past experiences to define me.

Throughout our discussion I made sure to validate that I knew he could do the same and he, like all of us, was deserving of love and respect. When I got up to leave he put out his hand and I took it in acknowledgement. He smiled and his eyes brimmed with tears, "Thank you CJ, I think I can do this." "I know you can Michael," I said, "you're a warrior."

Later that day we finally found placement for Michael, a VA in-patient situation where he could begin his recovery work. When it was time to go he again held out his hand in thanks. He was smiling, his eyes wet again. He nodded to me with no words to express what he was feeling. "Go make it a great life Michael. I'll be thinking about you and supporting you from afar to be strong. Take care." And so we said good-by.

Heart-felt connection with people is one of the simplest joys of life, and therapeutic communication is at the heart of nursing brilliantly. Science is now proving that when patients feel connection, healing is enhanced and we can measure the influx of "feel good" neurochemicals.

Achieving connection lies in discerning our commonalities with others. We, and our patients, gain strength to overcome challenges because we realize we are not struggling alone. At the time I met Michael, I was going through some difficult family stuff and hadn't felt confident in how to approach it. Genuinely connecting with him, hearing his story and the telling a bit of my story was a powerful experience which helped us both.

Though Michael's situation was an extreme case, it is a common human worry to question if we can succeed or are worthy. Circumstances can feel so overwhelming that we hide in shame and become hesitant to ask for help when we truly need it most, or we desperately try to connect, only to repel others with our desperation. When we are unable to see options, it can even propel us to suicidal thoughts or violence. The end result for any of these strategies is the same—self-imposed isolation.

Connection with others is a deep, human need. Remember, our very DNA is structured to identify in a tribal sense and that wiring is why we find comfort in connection. The extremes are where we can lose ourselves and become expatriates of our own tribes, believing isolation is safer than connection.

Sadly too, as a result of all the crazy stuff going on in the world, we try to connect only with those we know and trust, thinking we have to know and trust to really connect—not true. Some also believe connection takes a significant time investment, which implies a busy life allows for only a few true connections—also not true. The result is a shrinking of community and a pervasive increased sense of isolation. As the belief that we share few commonalities with others continues, the distance between us grows. Sometimes, hostility toward anyone seemingly different from us can happen resulting in racism, prejudice, random violence, etc. In my own experience, this misguided belief and resulting protection of self could not be further from the truth.

Connecting with people does not require special circumstances, extensive self-disclosure or significant time investment. Connection happens when we are mindful—utilizing that mental state of being fully present in the moment, are less self-absorbed and in a mindset of knowing we contribute to the whole experience of life. It also seems the more mindful I become, the less time it takes to achieve connection. In fact, when I am truly mindful, it takes almost no time at all to gain connection. Being mindful when with others—strangers or familiars—we become more capable of sensing another's current state. Connection is always possible when in the presence of another human being, we just have to embrace it in the context of the moment.

One of the simplest ways we can connect is through acts of service, when we fill some sort of need for another. Just opening a door for someone has the potential to connect with others. Acts of courtesy like this can demonstrate we see ourselves as part of a community, whether we know each other or not. Even in brief moments like that an exchange occurs. An infusion, if you will, of each person's goodwill and empathy, it conveys a sense we are all in this together. Both will benefit—the giver gains in his or her sense of purpose and the receiver recognizes he or she belongs. This is how true connection through serving others works.

Connection is a cornerstone of fostering excellence in healthcare because it enhances our ability to effectively support and mentor both patients and colleagues. Relationships are enriched as true interest in another's well-being is expressed. In our connection, we mutually seek to cooperate, and this is why the effort to connect and to serve has the potential to augment any relationship we choose.

In our roles as healthcare providers, it can also be powerful to draw on our own experience of pain or illness as we relate to patients. When we incorporate where we share common ground into our practice, whether we verbalize what they are or just draw on them, our communication becomes more genuine. On the surface we may not think we have anything in common with the disheveled homeless person before us, but in honest assessment of our own history, can we really say we have never spent any time in a dark place where we could not see options? He or she may not have the will to change course, but approaching from even the tiniest bit of relatable experience is the best start for creating connection and positive impact. It is one of the greatest tests of our character to remember that even badly behaving people desire underneath it all, at very least, the same thing we do—caring and respect.

As practitioners, connection adds to our sense of purpose because in our openness and empathy, we increase awareness of our influence and ability to make the world a better place. When we interact with patients in ways that reveal our humanity, we remember our struggles are not unique to us. With this heightened awareness and embrace of our own humanness, the fears of not being enough also begin to dissipate and we feel greater purpose and satisfaction in our work.

Connection won't happen with everyone, and some days you will be better at it than others, but making the effort to meet people where they are is one of the ways our patients judge the quality of their care. It was a very observant and experienced EMS worker named Thom Dick who shared that people don't remember much about our medical expertise, but they do remember their emotional response to it and how well we did or didn't assist them through their difficult experience. Whether we are connecting as a coworker, patient or friend, the greatest impact we have on people is the emotional response we evoke and the feelings others have when we leave them. Even if we judge a person's emotional state to be chaotic, inappropriate or unreasonable, the smart provider knows that in order to manage toward something better, we have to put the judgment aside and begin with whatever current state and perceptions are presented. We are a service industry and often challenged with folks who are not at their best because they are sick, scared, or otherwise disordered. It is a reasonable patient expectation that we have the professionalism to be mindful and empathetic when assisting them toward a more positive state of physical and emotional well-being.

C. J. Snow

The Barriers Of Judgment And Perception

In our work with patients, we often attach all sorts of judgments, interpretations and feelings to them without even realizing it. Sometimes we only give our best to those we feel deserve it and withhold parts of our best selves from those we feel don't. Perhaps a patient reminds us of our former dead-beat boy-friend, our neglectful mother, or some narcissistic addict we've encountered. Because of our judgments, we can feel energized and pleased with those we pronounce worthy or end up feeling exhausted and irritable when caring for those we consider unde-serving. Withholding all or some of who we are as caregivers leaves everyone feeling shorted.

The problem with this unconscious judgmental approach is two-fold. First, people generally sense judgmental attitudes and will often reflexively gravitate to a defensive position, limiting our effectiveness and taking way more time and effort to work with effectively. Second, we will fail in connecting with them and by default lose out on the satisfaction of feeling purposeful and making a difference with that patient. Our conscience and self-judgment will on some level recognize the lack of compas-sion, misaligned with our expressed values and we will feel the worse for it. Decent people simply cannot feel good about being unkind or neglectful. We can never predict the full impact of our focused kindness and compassion on another person. Our contribution may just be the tipping point for positive change.

Taking a moment to listen to a patient's, coworker's, or spouse's perspective is the most basic and powerful way to connect and show we care. Our attention is perhaps the most important thing we offer another. When people feel we've lis-tened to their concerns, given them a few moments of our time and acknowledged their experience, they will feel valued and heard. The gift of time and attention resonates! Every human has those basic needs of receiving love and respect. If we can provide even a smidgen of those, we will succeed in experienc-ing a degree of connection. It felt like magic when I started to understand this in my own practice. It was a bit startling to hear how my patients began describing their experience. I had been praised before as an excellent nurse, but it wasn't until I got this part that it became my frequent experience to have patients verbalize true, heart-felt appreciation for how they felt under my care. This is not to say I always am able to practice at this level, but the experience of nursing is transformed when I do. Work stops being quite so hard. The more I practice it, the easier it becomes to do this with consistency.

Sometimes Connection Doesn't Happen

It can be disappointing when we can't seem to get on the right track of communication with someone. Every individual has the freedom to respond in various ways to circumstances and many times other stressors get in the way of effective connection. Remembering this when we fail to connect with people will help to keep us from taking it personally. Sometimes emotions run high and displaced anger finds its way to you. Remember we always have choices about how we respond, both internally and to the person before us. Others may try to make us feel bad, but we don't have to take the bait. We all carry the dual responsibility of doing our best to evoke a positive response in others *and* to manage our own feelings and emotions. Eleanor Roosevelt wisely said, "No one can make you feel inferior without your consent."

Many people believe others do have power to make them feel a certain way (victim thinking,) but this can be used to our advantage. We can direct our interactions toward the desired outcome by letting others know how we *want them* to feel. Conversations often go much better, particularly if they are confrontational, if we state the positive outcome we hope to achieve at the very beginning. In my own practice, part of my self-introduction to a patient covers this point and it is how I like to start any difficult conversation. It is powerful to let people know we want to resolve problems with them, that we want them to feel cared for and their experience is important to us. Even if the person proves to be unreachable or the outcome misses the mark, we can be satisfied we gave it our best.

While we can and should cultivate connection and positive outcomes, we do not possess the power to control another person's response. We become less reactive and more deliberately responsive with this knowledge, which increases our skill in dealing with others and helps us avoid getting hooked by a person's negativity when things don't go as well as we had hoped for.

Connection with others is how we remember the world is bigger than ourselves. We are not isolated and separate. It is "our own optical delusion" as Albert Einstein put it, to think that we are. When we begin to experience our commonalities with others, our compassion grows and what follows is our integration with all that is around us. In this way we feel we belong. Our selfishness diminishes and that wonderful sense of being part of something greater expands. Loneliness and lack of purpose cannot exist in this connected place. Peace prevails. We become the best of who we are and our personal brand of excellence, as we roam about the world, grows.

···18···

Attitude Is Altitude

"You cannot always control what happens to you, but you can control your attitude towards what happens to you, and in that, you will be mastering change rather than allowing it to master you."

Brian Tracy

WHEN WE LET go of judging others, when we begin to know we are enough simply by offering our best and we focus on what we can control, choosing a positive attitude and a happy disposition is easier. More peace lives here too. Attitude and perspective toward our experiences is *always* (a word I do not use lightly) a choice.

What perspective we decide on has the power to elevate or depress. We say, "But they made me ..." or, "I'm in a bad mood because of..." Reality check! No one makes us do or feel anything; we always are—either consciously or unconsciously—the originator of our feelings and responses to things, people and events. That kind of ownership can be challenging.

Experiences are subject to interpretation and we have the opportunity to consciously design and control what our responses will be. I have been on the receiving end of some pretty egregious treatment, but in hindsight, wish I had chosen a different attitude when forming my response. Though I could find many supporters to say my response was justified, my chosen attitude did not elevate me or take me any nearer to what I really wanted.

Most people just want from us our best and do not expect perfection. It is a relief to both employers and spouses when we respond positively to correction and are open to feedback. Managers and life partners have varying degrees of skill, and we may not always like how correction is delivered, but I have learned that giving a big fat pause before responding is helpful and that resisting my natural urge to defend myself allows me to respond in a way that optimizes my circumstances. Organizations have their agendas, so do our partners. It is expected we fulfill or at least entertain them since one pays us and the other we are committed to. We may not always agree, but insisting on our own way can become a source of failure and blind us to other avenues leading to positive change.

Attitudes of negativity can also become habitual. Negativity is a small-minded perspective that is completely zeroed-in on the flaws of life. The focus can be so intense that positive things simultaneously occurring are completely missed. Negativity can be past-focused on things and events that peeved us, or future focused on the things that worry us and any attention to the current moment is dedicated to finding its flaws. Worse yet when negativity is coupled with the belief that things will never change, is a deep kind of cynicism that precedes despair. It robs us of happiness.

A positive attitude, on the other hand, is expansive. The perspective is broader, inclusive of all that is occurring and has a propensity to consciously savor the good stuff we experience. Gratitude and optimism are dominant in this state and enhance the ability to be fully present in the moment. These are reasons *possibility* abounds with a positive attitude—we have the altitude to see life from a higher perspective. Disappointments are not all consuming, but proportional, and they cease to overshadow things because we see so much more than the flaws.

That all being said, there may be bosses or partners who are easily threatened or have a need to control others in an excessive way. Surviving them can be difficult. There are times where it can feel like a defeat if we have to concede to the person with a bigger stick or give in to a partner who is unbending, wrong though we feel they may be. It behooves us to keep in mind that it's not our job to fix anyone else, we can only try to fix ourselves and become examples of what we want to experience in return. Others do learn by observing.

Sometimes circumstances persist and then become choice points. We either remove ourselves, invest in creating change, or find a way to accept things as they are. Whatever our choice, it is imperative the choice be made and executed with a positive perspective—our mental health depends on it. When we move decisively forward with optimism in an effort to create better than before, we can thrive, stay focused and on track with the life we want, even if it seems we lost a battle.

No matter what the end result—stay, leave, get promoted or perhaps even get fired—I find things have an odd way of working out for the best. If we maintain an attitude to do our best, with all we have, from where we are, it always has the potential to elevate us from current circumstances. It gives us new perspective and opportunity, even if some aspects of our story look like failure.

The point is, not all days at the job or in relationships are going to be great. Does that mean we are failing to achieve a level of happiness, practicing with excellence or not living out our dreams? No, it just means we have not had an excellent day, the job wasn't a good fit or the relationship needs a little work. Take the lessons with you, leave the day behind and strive for a better experience tomorrow. And if being positive is not coming naturally at the moment, "fake it 'til you make it." Even a pretend positive attitude has been shown to create a more optimistic perspective. Positivity is a life-benefitting trait to be cultivated and a positive attitude gives us the altitude to see things anew.

••• 19 •••

Surviving Tragedies And The Importance Of Resilience And Outlook

"All you need to know to stitch it together is to start in just one place where the knot will hold."

Anne Lamott

AND THEN THERE'S the harder stuff, things that eat at us, tap into our emotions or perhaps shake us to our core. Careers like ours can expose us to the harsh realities of life a bit more often than most, and life itself can have a myriad of stressors and difficulties. I have witnessed my share of tragic events, endured many of life's humiliations and disappointments, and I know I am not unique in that regard. So how do we manage the stress? What do we do to mitigate the effects of difficult experiences? How do we keep the haunting events out of our head? In other words, how do we recover and reset?

Some would advise to just put aside any emotional content when dealing with or resetting after an experience, the idea being we should completely separate our emotional selves from events. While medicine demands a degree of objectivity and we cannot allow our emotional responses to run amuck, we cannot fully separate from the emotional self. Feeling is part of being a decent human, it would be sociopathic to be devoid of feeling. As professionals, we benefit when we develop a level of self-awareness that notices when we are having emotional responses to events so we can deal with them effectively, yet still accept them as part of our human experience. How we share experiences and connect as humans through them is an important part of life. We may stubbornly and ardently deny the influence of feelings and make believe they are not having influence, but unrecognized or unresolved emotions from events can control our lives in insidious ways. Everyone must do their own work to process the taxing experiences that life throws at us. Looking at things in their naked rawness is where we can begin to understand how they have shaped who we are at this moment. But we can't stop there. If we do, we may find ourselves believing we are the way we are because of them, like it is some kind of fixed outcome. To stay stuck there is a victim mentality. We must work to go beyond the experiences that wound us. We have to decide how we want those experiences to shape our current and future life in constructive ways.

As an example of this, for many years of my adult life I was stuck in the story of my childhood trauma. When I was twelve, both my parents shifted from being the stereotypical parents of a nuclear family, to self-absorbed, "Do your own thing" people of the '70s. The safety of my secure and predictable family life disintegrated almost overnight. My Dad moved out, our home was sold and my Mom bought a one-bedroom condo 250 miles away. My Dad had a two-bedroom house frequented by his girlfriend where my two brothers and I suddenly found ourselves living. I felt like an extraneous component, sleeping on his couch, and didn't really know where I fit in anymore. I did what many kids do, I found myself getting into lots of trouble stemming from what I perceived as rejection and abandonment.

Fortunately, I narrowly escaped a life damaged by drug abuse and persuaded my parents to allow me to go to boarding school at age fourteen. It was an unusual setting within a spiritually based commune with only seven students enrolled in the high school. It was unconventional, but in addition to my studies I learned to garden, milk cows, cook in the centralized kitchen for large groups of people and was fortunate enough to have many kind people look after me. It was a secure environment with people who loved me like family and they helped me to heal. In spite of the almost three years I spent there, my childhood trauma re-emerged when I left. At seventeen I moved to southern California and began supporting myself and attending junior college. Though things were going well, I sometimes found myself feeling deeply resentful. I did my best to be positive and productive and had many successes, but there was an underlying anger, mostly unconscious, overshadowing everything that only grew as time passed. This generated more fears of rejection and abandonment, troublesome behaviors and continual worries about my capabilities that recurrently affected many aspects of my life. I did not hold myself accountable for how I behaved, I made excuses by explaining the story of that twelve year old girl. It was a belief I couldn't help being the way I was *because of that experience*. That ineffective strategy kept me stuck and making lots of mistakes. I was still living in an old story from a completely entrenched victim perspective. It's important to note here that while I am using my childhood trauma to illustrate the point, many of us have adult experiences that have similar effects, coloring other experiences through the lens of the past rather than seeing things clearly in current context.

My personal route in overcoming this encompassed a variety of things; meditation, personal development work (seminars, counseling, books, etc.) and writing. With these tools I was able to bring that challenging upbringing into positive perspective, embrace the strengths it gave me and truly appreciate my ability to be resilient. It also gave me the ability to forgive my parents and liberate me from the subtle anger I had been carrying for so long. Now I have a better handle on how those long-ago experiences can be leveraged to my advantage and I use those same skills when managing difficulties I encounter now. Though a bit painful to do the work initially, I learned that I have to fully embrace and accept my experiences, not stay stuck in the disappointment or injustice of it. I have to look at experiences honestly and own my part of how I respond to them if I want to work through the negativity and have them work to my benefit.

Whatever course we choose in our lives and careers, there will occasionally be occurrences and places that seem dark, harrowing and touch us at a very deep level. Many of us work to protect ourselves from such things or scramble to get as far away as possible from those experiences, burying them, thinking it will cease to affect our lives if we do. But somewhere in our neurology the experience is remembered and life will inevitably bring difficult circumstances that dig them up, regardless of the safeguards we have placed around us. If we respond according to our past experiences, which remain unilluminated and without learning, we rarely choose the most helpful responses.

Over the years I have watched many healthcare providers operate in a fashion devoid of any feeling. This may create some sense of safety for the caregiver, but the flaw is that we, in effect, emotionally abandon our patients at a time when they need a bit of humanness or that touch of compassionate care demonstrating we are human and capable of feelings. This "hard core" strategy devoid of feeling is most commonly found in the critical-care arenas where we can find tough, seemingly uncaring providers. Forgive them. They have yet to learn a more humane way to cope, one where they can manage their responses to events and still show compassion and their human side without feeling depleted or inappropriate. We can learn to be vulnerable and open with our feelings, yet professionally appropriate and psychologically safe at the same time.

Warts And All

Knowing ourselves and embracing those less than pretty parts of us gives us the clarity to rise above them. For example, if you suffered any sort of abuse in your past, it is likely you would be reactive to caring for an abused woman or the abuser because you have personal experience and judgments about the issue. That is natural and justified because it gives you discernment so you can avoid future abuse. I'm just suggesting that knowing what our judgments are and understanding how they can be helpful or create barriers is worth exploring if we wish to gain mastery over them and be the best at what we do. Doing so enables us to be optimally effective and resilient at work and in our relationships. It's a critical piece of finding that sweet-spot as professionals.

Evaluation of how we show up in life is a "warts and all" process. It takes raw honesty to achieve self-mastery. We also must remember to be kind to ourselves, knowing that where we are is where to begin the work, not a place of disappointment that we are not all we hoped to be. As we start to better know ourselves and how our life experiences and beliefs have shaped us, we are better prepared to manage those things capable of triggering a reaction, or perhaps more capable in our work because we can relate on a personal level and can share what we learned. With this effort, we become more authentic in our responses and do so in ways that align with the self we aspire to, rather than acting on old patterns or beliefs. Knowing ourselves this way gives us the necessary objectivity to be resilient, and to have a more positive, constructive outlook. And here's an added bonus: these qualities of resilience and a positive outlook are, research tells us, the two most predominant strengths of happy people.

So What Is Your Perspective On Death?

Life has the inescapable element of death. We all eventually have to deal with it, and in medicine it is likely to come sooner than later. I have been at the side of many people as death came. It is expected to encounter it more frequently in the Emergency Department, my flight nurse job and the ICU. Many of them had additional tragic elements to their stories making the death even more heart wrenching. The ability to remain effective, therapeutic and resilient in dealing with death requires a degree of comfort with it. When we take the time to process our beliefs and feelings about death, we can reduce some of the emotional charge around it, which allows us to stay clear of the blinding emotional hooks when circumstances poke at our own fears of how unpredictable life can be. Having a philosophical structure around death allows me to remain emotionally available for my patients and their families when death is imminent or has occurred. For me, my spiritual beliefs are the scaffolding for accepting death. I believe we are more than our physical body and that we don't "end" when the physical body gives out. Every practitioner must discover for themselves what their structures are. However you chose to view death, what is most important is to manage our own fear of death and be comfortable with its inevitability. If we are afraid of death, it will translate into our work. It is difficult to assist the dying or the people left behind if we are hooked by our own fear. My personal beliefs provide a solid platform on which to manage my own emotions, and therefore assist them as they manage theirs. There is always room to include our humanness. It's okay to feel, it's okay to share tears with the family and it is often therapeutic to do so if the emotion is honest and heartfelt, generated by your empathy. It's when we don't allow our feelings and authentic responses to surface that the suppressed emotions can have unintended impact, like the emotional abandonment of our patients and families or the depletion of our strength as caregivers.

Dealing with circumstances in an authentic way, allowing space for emotion to be felt, gives us the ability to move on. It is like the martial artist who is able to take the energy of a charging opponent and transfer that energy into an action disabling the opponent. When we stop resisting the battle before us and fully dance with it, we transform the experience into something powerful and meaningful. While we cannot fully control a patient's outcome and survival, we can influence how that outcome is experienced, which in turn may powerfully alter how it affects those experiencing it with us.

Decompression And Perception Management

There has been lots of talk about Critical Incident Stress Management (CISM) and incorporating it into our working lives. In my experience, formal CISM rarely gets deployed. Only with really big events do we consider it, while many smaller events chip away at our well-being. We are often left to our own devices to manage our stress, and sometimes that comes in the form of alcohol, drugs and other unhealthy habits.

We may have beliefs we should be "tough," "professional," and "able to process" difficult events. The truth is that none of us are able to do this effectively 100% of the time, no matter how much personal work and reflection we do. This is where Critical Event debriefing and being part of a supportive team can be helpful. True, structured and professionally led CISM for significant events is critical, but it is not always necessary to carry it out in a formal way for smaller events. We can support each other through informal CISM principles where our listening ears, our empathy, our kind words and gentle hugs can be helpful to all of us.

One exceptionally important principle we have come to understand regarding managing stress through debriefing, is the importance of doing so *before* we sleep. We now know the human psyche subconsciously processes events while we sleep and this is how they become part of our long-term experience in the form of beliefs, fears, ineffective coping mechanisms, etc. Managing them prior to the brain doing its own work is helpful because we can put the events in an appropriate context so that distortions, which can occur both in our misperceptions of events and through distortions that occur in dream state, are mitigated to a significant degree. Part of this processing may be to acknowledge we did the best we could with what we knew and perhaps that some elements may have been beyond our control. The effort to reframe things to a positive perspective, even if the only positive is that we learned something, builds rather than dismantles our psyche. This is why you will find portions of this book recommending various ways to do our own debriefings at the end of the day, like the self-debrief I've described on my way home.

Guard Against Negative Debriefings

Debriefings with negative spins depress our psyche. I used to go home and complain about all that went wrong during my day. It was innocently intended and I thought I was decompressing, but obsession with the negative and a blaming mentality is not healthy. My husband was a patient listener, but I found myself noticing how awful it all sounded—the peevish recollections of my experiences and the harsh judgments about others and the rantings of how things should be. Moreover, it was NOT the best way to reconnect with the love of my life at the end of the day, and I noticed the impact on our relationship.

I often think about how the happy and successful people I have admired in my life are not complainers. They just aren't. They focus on the wins and that is what keeps them fueled to tackle the difficulties life dishes out and keeps them propelled toward better. They do not think of the things that didn't work out as hopeless failures, they looked at them as learning opportunities. There's little drama, it's just another day unfolding. They put their new experiential knowledge to work for them so their approach tomorrow will be wiser still. Many of us look at our seeming failures as the "junk" in our lives and don't want to look at them any longer than we have to or would rather ignore them all together. But as Edison put it—and I just love this— "To invent, you need a good imagination AND a pile of junk." And such is life. We are indeed "inventing" our lives as we live it, utilizing what's been learned from the junk.

Being even-keeled about things and never getting over-elated or greatly worried about circumstances is another great practice to employ. Here is a fable I once heard that is such a great allegory for this:

> A man and his family lived on a farm. One day his prize stallion ran away and despite extensive searching, he could not be found. "Oh, dear! What a tragedy!" empathized his friends. "Oh, maybe, maybe not," he replied, "we shall see." The next day the stallion returned and with him several beautiful mares. "Oh what good fortune!" a friend said. "Maybe, maybe not," said the man, "we shall see." The next day his son, a skilled horseman, began training the new wild horses. He was bucked off and broke his leg. "Oh mercy!" said his friend, "that is a terrible calamity!" "Maybe, maybe not" the wise farmer replied. That week a troop of the king's men rode through the town, requiring all the young men to go to war. The farmer's son was not considered because of his injury. The rest of the men went to battle and not a one survived.

Life is full of the unexpected. Being even-keeled preserves our energy for whatever new action is needed to keep us moving in the right direction. This kind of adaptability and resilience is how many of the truly great captured their success, even in the context of setbacks.

As healthcare providers, we have the privilege of taking care of people, making decisions, and offering advice to help people heal. There are few jobs that can offer such a sacred and impactful responsibility. Celebrate and be grateful for what you are able to do. Be passionate about doing more and help each other to be more, and like the farmer, don't get too rattled by the unexpected and avoid the drama. This way you will then have less to decompress from.

Keeping this well-rounded perspective is a powerful thing and its focus can add to our satisfaction and reserve energy for other pursuits. Simply put, when things don't turn out as you hoped, humbly put them in your pile of junk so you can use it later to create something extraordinary.

Not all live life with a high level of self-awareness and the tools to navigate sticky points, so don't be afraid to reach out to those you think may be struggling. Bring what you can to the table, support each other and make your own debriefs a habit after critical events or disturbing experiences. We all have times where we have to pull ourselves together or must support others to do the same. When we do it with clarity, kindness and love, we can do as Anne Lamott suggests: we find the *"one place where the knot will hold"*...and carry on.

···20···

Thresholds And Breaking Points

"If you can't fly then run, if you can't run then walk, if you can't walk then crawl but whatever you do you have to keep moving forward."

Martin Luther King, Jr.

IN THE SCIENTIFIC world, the term threshold means; *the magnitude or intensity that must be exceeded for a certain reaction, phenomenon, result, or condition to occur or be manifested.* As humans, we have thresholds in a biological sense that result in biochemical changes and in our psyche causing changes to our mind and spirit. These changes are of an endless variety and can last for a few moments to many years. Some can be a complete undoing where recovery is a long, slow road.

Often we do not know what will trigger an arrival at our thresholds until we are staring one in the face—the perfect constellation of circumstances occurs and there it is. Thresholds are places where we suddenly find ourselves unable to effectively cope, physically and/or mentally, with what is before us. Our ineffectiveness can be subtle or overt, with a wide range of presentations, some as subtle as becoming impatient or losing our temper, others so big they change our lives with long-lasting effects, like with Post-Traumatic Stress Disorder. We all have thresholds—even if we have yet to experience one big enough to really grab our attention—and we all have our individual capacities as to how much we can handle.

Thresholds can also fluctuate depending on the context of our lives. A person who has just recently lost a spouse or a job is likely not to be as adaptive with challenges; or conversely, a person who just returned from a relaxing vacation may be able to absorb a lot more. Both balance in how we live our lives and mindfulness are tools that enhance our resilience, our happiness, our ability to endure, which keep our thresholds high.

Understanding and learning to recognize our personal warning signs of ineffectual coping are much like knowing how to read signs on the road we are traveling. If we pay attention to those signs, understand them and respond to them, we are less likely to get lost or be injured in our travels. Common signs of ineffectual coping include fitful sleep, drinking alcohol in excess, smoking, overeating, drug use, increasingly frequent headaches, skin rashes and many illnesses can be attributed to stress. Recognizing these behaviors and physical responses for what they are and acting on the apparent need to implement some countermeasures can be life-saving, marriage-saving and happiness-preserving. We have to recognize the signs and intervene in healthy ways when we see them.

Thresholds can also be exceeded when life presents a perfect storm of events, where we have little time to mitigate during the on rushing cascade of events. Some of us may never encounter events that rock us to our core, but believing that we will never meet one is naive.

Throughout my career I have consistently thrived in stressful environments and have historically bounced back from hardship. I have seen horrific things in my line of work, experienced some very difficult things in my life, yet am typically happy, enjoy my life, and am free from any destructive habits. I consider myself pretty tough and would describe myself as having a resilient psyche and adaptive to adversity. So when I met my own thresh-old and toppled over to a breaking point, it took me completely by surprise, and took me down hard.

Thinking back, I now understand the constellation of events that exceeded at my threshold began a couple of months prior to the actual day of my undoing. It was during my first year of training as a flight nurse. The job was far more demanding than I had ever experienced in my career, and this stressful context was the backdrop for the subsequent events. The first event occurred on a hot summer day while I was taking a safety nap, something allowed for twenty-four hour shift workers. I was awakened by the radio dispatch requesting our flight team to respond to a law enforcement helicopter crash. Shaking off the sleep, my first thought was, "Did I hear that right?" Throughout our relatively short flight to the scene we were unusually quiet, intently listening to the ground radio traffic from fire and law enforcement, giving details to the responders about where to go, how to control the resulting brush fire and their work to con-trol the public. Particularly unusual was the palpable emotion in the voices of the scene commanders, who are normally some-what factual and flat in voice tone. It became clear, even before our arrival, that what had occurred was a devastating event.

This was way beyond the normal chaos inherent in the EMS world: things feel upside-down when the victims involved are part of our extended family. On our arrival there were more law enforcement, firefighters, and paramedics in one place than we normally see. Throughout my career, law enforcement has been a rock-solid presence that had protected me and kept me safe both in the emergency department and on the streets in my EMS fieldwork. But what I was witnessing here felt disorient-ing and the collective grief was palpable. I had never imagined my brethren's faces and voices so pained and unfamiliar. It was understandable because uniformed personnel had been aboard; all of them were in terrible shape.

As we joined in the care of the pilot, whom I'll call Sam, I was immediately confronted with the severity of his injuries. It was clear Sam was gone. Not even a trauma room appearing in the parking lot where we were would have been able to save him, yet the whole group was invested in doing everything possible. Even though it was contrary to our policy to fly a non-viable patient, we made the decision to transport him. We knew it would be of value for all of us to feel everything that could be done was being done for one of our own. We could not leave this man, who had so often offered his help to others at great personal risk, lying in a parking lot waiting for the coroner. After turning Sam over to the trauma team at the hospital, we were walking out and I saw an older woman, crying and walking with others toward the trauma bay. Her facial features were so similar to Sam's that I realized she was his mother. I remember thinking, "My God, I cannot imagine the level of grief she feels."

After the sad and quiet flight back to base, my partner and I went back to routine, completing paperwork, house duties, etc. I did get a call from my supervisor to see if we wanted to go home, but we thought we were fine so we finished the shift somberly, but without a "problem" like the "professionals" we were expected to be. What I know now is that after being involved in an event of such magnitude, we are poor judges of our need to process and we should have sought out a full debrief to support our processing.

I ended up going to my chiropractor the next morning after work for a routine adjustment (back pain being what I now know to be one of my tells when I am reaching the limits of my coping strategies) and in the process of getting worked on I suddenly, seemingly out of nowhere, had a crying jags like I might have had when I was five years old. I just couldn't stop. I had been doing EMS work for decades by this point and never had a response like this. It was completely involuntary and came with a deep ache that felt like it would tear open my chest. Fortunately, my chiropractor was a good healer and a kind man who helped me process my grief. I was able to go home and get the much-needed rest that had eluded me the night before.

The funeral services for Sam helped to give me additional closure, but I still felt bereft for a long time, like a subtle undercurrent disturbing me from the inside out. I suppose part of it was I had a greater appreciation for the realities of an airborne job, how we are all vulnerable and it struck close to home. I had asked to attend the law enforcement's Critical Incident Stress Management session, but they thought it best only their guys attend which was understandable. I was offered assistance by my employer, but I thought I could handle it in my own way. I did my best to cope privately with the event and to keep my life on track and I thought I was doing okay.

A few days later I was contacted by email by the officer who was beside me performing CPR on Sam. He wanted to thank me for doing our best. My response to him ended up as a long, heart-felt response, expressing how difficult it was for me to see one of my "protectors" and a "warrior for good" lose his life, and how difficult it was to be incapable of changing the outcome. Unbeknownst to me, he shared my email with other law enforcement and Sam's mother. It touched others deeply. Sharing with him the experience from my perspective, resulted in further healing and friendships with other members of the department. We became united in a friendship which found an outlet to do charity work for a local children's hospital. What touched me most was when I received a card in the mail, accompanied by a nurse-angel statue that was sent from Sam's mother to express her gratitude for my words and for tending to her son. That angel still has a place of honor on my bookshelf to remind me that healing comes in ways unexpected, especially when we give from the heart.

I went on with life and work, but I didn't take enough stock of the fact that I was still healing. It was like recovering from an injury where one can forget it is still healing because it feels pretty good. But if pressed too hard, that healing injury may become something catastrophic. I was just beginning to feel more like my old self when the trifecta I mentioned at the beginning of the book happened. It had been a long career, I had seen a lot of disturbing stuff, yet nothing had catapulted me past my threshold the way this series of events did.

It was several months after the law enforcement helicopter crash. I was working with my regular partner, pulling a forty-eight hour shift. Our first response request came early in the day. It involved a small child whose parents were washing their car, the brake failed and the car ran her over. When we arrived, she was in severe distress. Her abdomen, complete with distinct tire marks, was growing larger and firmer, and her level of consciousness was falling to a state where she was responsive only to pain. Upon loading her in the helicopter, I asked my partner to begin setting up for Rapid Sequence Intubation (RSI) to protect her airway. On commencement of RSI, all went well until I tried to insert the endotracheal tube. Though the size tube we used for her came straight out of standard medical guidelines, her airway was too narrow, and I was unable to pass the tube. This delay and the increasing abdominal pressure caused her stomach content to empty into her airway. It was not something thin and liquid, easily cleared with suction, but thick like oatmeal, and clearing the airway for our second attempt was difficult. I was able to insert a second tube a half-size smaller but it became clogged with the aspirate. At this point we were landing at the receiving facility and managed her airway in basic life support fashion.

When we brought her to the trauma room, the team took over. We felt very disheartened over our failed airway attempt, well aware the anoxia caused by the aspiration and our inability to clear it would be consequential if she survived. She died before they could even get her to the operating room.

We had the required discussion with our Medical Director, a requirement any time there were unexpected complications, and he spoke with the trauma team. As is somewhat common in highly emotional events like pediatric trauma and the loss of a patient, the team had contacted him and was in full blame mode, saying that our failed attempts to control her airway contributed to her cause of death. It was very stressful and difficult to hear them blaming us for "contributing" to such a horrible thing. We genuinely felt that we had done everything we could for her but encountered insurmountable difficulties. It was somewhat consoling when, a week later, the coroner notified our Medical Director saying her death was caused by the "loss of blood in her abdomen from her non-survivable liver injury."

My partner, who had his own young daughter of the same age at home, was so upset he could not complete his shift. I remained at work, sad but knowing I had done my absolute best to help that child survive.

A relief medic came in to cover for my partner. We ran multiple calls that day and into the night, but on the following day, we had another pediatric trauma call. This child was a bit older than the first. He was riding in the front seat with his grandfather when the car was hit squarely on the driver's side at a high rate of speed. When I got into the back of the ambulance on scene, I had difficulty making sense of what I was seeing. The ferrous smell of blood was intense and the child was covered in large clots of blood, but I could see his skin color was normal, not pale the way it would be with blood loss. I asked the firefighter standing outside the ambulance, "Where did all this blood come from?" He told me the grandfather had been decapitated and found dead on the child's lap. Those words chilled me to the bone as my brain automatically visualized the scene, but I had a job to do so I climbed in the ambulance to assess him.

Physically he did not appear to be injured, but I will never forget his face and what it expressed. He was so emotionally impacted by this horrific event he would not respond to any of my questions or even look at me. My assessment told me he didn't seem to have physical or neurological injury. Tears steadily ran down his blood-spattered face and his staring blankly straight ahead went straight to my heart as I thought of the impact this event would likely have on his life. We talked to him and reassured him continually while in our care. He stopped crying, but was still not talking when we turned him over to the trauma team.

Pony-up and get back to base, right? There was a report to write. I went to my bunk at midnight and fell into a dead-tired sleep. I was awakened by a 5:00 AM call. A car had run off the highway and into a tree sometime during the night. At that point I was about forty-six hours into my shift. I had slept a total of about nine hours between the two nights, but I was used to this and felt ready to go, as usual.

When we arrived on the scene I could see firefighters gathered around a toddler still strapped in a car seat. Kneeling beside them, I took report from the medic. It had been a cold night and it was apparent the crash had happened several hours before given the dewy frost on the car. He told me the mother was in the front seat and had been deceased for some time. He thought the toddler was not injured, but she had spatters of mom's blood on her and tearstains on her face. Her lips were trembling as though still crying but dry of tears. I could see her shivering with cold under the blanket. I'm not sure why visuals always come to mind for me, but I flashed on what it must have been like for her alone, in the dark, cold, scared and desperately trying to get a response from her mother. Just at that moment she began to whimper and said, "Moooommmy" in the saddest little voice I have ever heard. That was the moment, my tipping point.

It was like a ton of bricks had buried me. I trembled like I caught a chill, my chest constricted and for what seemed like the longest moment of my life I could not breathe, tears welled up in my eyes, and for a moment I couldn't see. I distinctly remember the two firefighters kneeling beside me and putting my hands on their knees for strength I said, "Give me a minute guys."

I'm not sure how things would have gone had I not learned a centering technique at a conference a year or two prior. It's something that law enforcement and the military had been using to help settle the nerves and focus when in tense situations. It only takes a few seconds to deploy, is highly effective and I had been practicing it everywhere from calming down in heavy traffic to the stressful emergencies I encountered at work. I was fortunate it had become an automatic thing to use it at that moment to regain my composure. I finished the call, gave a professional turnover at the hospital, and then got on the phone to my boss. I requested to go home and for a temporary transfer to our fixed-wing base where the patients were of the less critical variety. We returned back to base, I packed up my gear and made some calls for emergency counseling. I felt some embarrassment over not being able to cope, but my coworkers were appropriately supportive as there was no denying I was in bad shape; I was repeatedly tearful, trembling at times and nauseated. Experiencing all three events up close and in a short amount of time, being slightly sleep-deprived, and suffering some unresolved distress over the law enforcement helicopter crash had created a constellation of circumstances that brought me to my breaking point.

On that morning in those circumstances, I reached the limits of my capacity to be resourceful. It took time, a willingness to deal with my vulnerabilities and some professional help to re-find my resilience. Many of the things I learned during my time of recovery are woven into this book. To this day the retelling of those events brings tears to my eyes, but today I experience those tears as an expression of strength, testimony to the building of my resilience and an honoring of those tragic events. I was able to return to the helicopter division a few months later and loved the seven years that followed as a flight nurse. I have witnessed many tragic events since that time. Thankfully I have not reached that threshold again; partly because I am wiser in managing stressors and do not allow them to accumulate; partly perhaps because the experience pushed my threshold higher; and partly because I have perhaps just been lucky.

I tell this story so you know what can happen, even to experienced and strong people. Sometimes it can be a singular event that has parallels in your own life that are too close for comfort. The event or events can bring up feelings of loss as if they were your own. My partner who went home after the first event, said he just needed to hug his daughter to assure himself she was okay. It may be just a singular event coupled with a current context of being ill or hormonal, adding to your lack of coping mechanisms under the circumstances. It may be a series of stressful events that compound each other as mine was. It will be different for everyone. Everyone has a tipping point. It's just a matter of whether or not circumstances conspire to route you there. Did you know that the primary causes of PTSD in the civilian population are traffic accidents and long ICU stays? It doesn't take a battlefield to tip our psyche to a point of overload.

What is important is this: that we remain vigilant for the appearance of distress, we monitor ourselves and our coworkers for indications that coping mechanisms are failing, and we are compassionate and smart enough to offer support and kind words to ourselves and others when we are affected. Sometimes, it may be appropriate to compassionately nudge others to seek professional guidance, even if they initially resist it. Even just a hug in the moment acknowledging things are difficult, or taking them someplace private to just breathe for a moment can be hugely impactful gestures to dissipate the stress and help others to stay resourceful.

Everyone struggles. Knowing that, accepting it as part of our humanity and being supportive of others or getting some help when needed fosters our resilience and helps us retain a positive outlook. That is how we care for ourselves, care for our coworkers, our patients and our families. It's a large factor in preventing burn out. Remembering that we are human, need balance, that some situations are just too much to bear alone, and that there is no shame in needing help and getting support—these things keep us from being depleted and vulnerable.

It is crucial to incorporate this bit of insight as we work in stressful environments and cope with a stressful world. Maintaining a life balanced by enjoyable activity, being vigilant for signs of human duress, and intervening early are how we can thrive in taxing careers, preserve our relationships and live a healthy, well-grounded life. With good self-care and a little luck, you may never have to face your own breaking point.

••• 21 •••

Use Change As Your Catalyst For More

"We can make the best or the worst of it. I hope you make the best of it. And I hope you see things that startle you. I hope you feel things you never felt before. I hope you meet people with a different point of view. I hope you live a life you're proud of. If you find that you're not, I hope you have the courage to start all over again."

Eric Roth screenplay,
The Curious Case of Benjamin Button

THEN ONE DAY, I got fired from the job I had been most proud of in my entire life. It was ten years into my flight nurse career, seven working for my company that had taught me so much about excellence, and I mistakenly believed my seniority and good standing would protect me. I had been experiencing a career high for several years—confident, skillful and respected. I loved my job and the synergy when working seamlessly with my paramedic partner and pilot when carrying out our missions was a routine high. Every day was a new adventure. It was a thrill I had rarely experienced in my nursing career and I savored it; but I think in retrospect the full truth was I had begun to take it for granted and began focusing too heavily on the flaws that I was seeing in my workplace, particularly in relation to my new boss. I was also ignoring the price I paid working twenty-four hour shifts, both in my health and in my marriage. I was fifty-four years old, and it was getting tough. These were all warning signs toward an untenable situation.

My company was growing rapidly and much to my distress I began to see our core values diminish in their visibility. Even my new boss, new to the company, seemed to have skipped the orientation class that focused on the heart of our company and the importance of integrity. I began pushing hard to return to our basics, but multiple factors led to my demise in this effort— mostly because I was too hard headed to realize the change I was seeking was beyond my control and insisting on it was equivalent to ignoring an oncoming train. Few life changes have impacted me to such a degree as being forced to separate from that company and career where I had fully invested my love of service and my passion for excellence.

Change can be a hard thing, especially if we are not fully pre-pared for it. We get comfortable in our circumstances and resent it if we find ourselves in a place that demands a change within us or adaptation to something not of our choosing. No one is likely to fault us for feeling this way. After all, who doesn't like being in a place where all is going reasonably well and we have our groove on because we've adapted nicely to how things are?

Most of us would agree that changes in life are inevitable. Yet, even though we are smart enough to know this is a sound truth, we find ourselves railing against change. A first response is often to resist it, ask why we need this change, and get busy thinking about all the reasons why we shouldn't change. It's rea-sonable to ask these questions, we want to understand, and we hope to agree. The trouble lies when we cannot achieve both understanding the circumstances and agreeing with it. So, what to do then?

The types of changes we face are of endless variety. Changes can be big or small, be about work life, on an internal level or on the home front. They may be a surprise or we may have seen them coming. We may initiate the change ourselves or have it imposed upon us. However it comes and whatever the variety, how we view change can result in our adaptation with grace and fluidity, or it can be messy and even tumultuous. So I would ask you; how do you want to handle this certainty of life, this unavoidable devil we call change? Cultivating a mindset that accepts change as part of life grooms us to be ready and adaptable when it comes.

It's helpful to remember first that many changes result outside our circle of influence or above our paygrade. Railing against something we have no control over is a waste of energy and emotion. Focus on what we can control—our attitudes and actions—so that we think, speak and act in ways that foster our best response to events, learning and adapting to the changing landscape. I'm not suggesting that we just roll-over with all changes that come our way, I'm only saying we should be thoughtful about how we spend our time and energy when they arrive. There may be courageous battles that need fighting, but choosing to fight takes wisdom and being effective takes careful evaluation to determine if we actually can be heard and if it's worth the effort. We also need ongoing evaluation of our actions and the response to know whether to stay the course, change strategy or change venue.

Change In The Work World

In the work world, we are often not part of the team initiating change yet we are responsible for following the directives given. Resentment over our subordinate position can build to the point of becoming a prevailing attitude, particularly when no efforts from leadership have been made for buy in. More of a "You're lucky I want to play along with this" rather than an "Okay, let's do this and see how it turns out," which is all that a reasonable boss would ask for when initiating change. Many organizations fail to fully consider a normal human response when attempting to implement change. They either lack transparency as to the why's and wherefores or they simply don't think of it as necessary to offer an explanation. These approaches seldom go well when the end-user is not involved and it creates more unrest than necessary when change is asked for. The smartest employers I have worked for practice transparency with change, warts and all, unafraid to share the flaws necessitating change. They display a willingness to adjust a plan if necessary. They treat their employees as intelligent, reasonable people by sharing the motives for change, then invite us along to see if the new plan provides the improvement desired. Communication continues up and down the chain of command until the desired result is achieved and the whole team is recognized as the victors of positive change.

Many of us do not work in such ideal organizations. I have found, however, if we are willing to partner with proposed change and give our best to it, we are more likely to be listened to if adjustments are needed. It has taken me some time to get to this perspective, but I have come to realize it as the most influential position I can adopt as a subordinate. Many folks, including myself for a number of years, would rather just complain and resist change. But think for a moment, do you really want to hang out with negativity and employ the extra effort it takes to swim against the current? I realized I don't. Even when it comes to the annoying stuff at work—you know, those things that seem to persist in spite of all the evidence that it is failing—I have a choice to make: just accept it and give it no more head space than necessary, create an avenue for changing it or determine the job is no longer desirable and move on.

Effective coping of this type is not blind acceptance, it means we speak to the dysfunction if opportunity arises and by all means endeavor to constructively advocate for what we believe to be a solution. Obsessively objecting to it will likely bear the consequence of earning the reputation of a bad attitude or being a difficult employee. Additionally, attitudes of resistance and pessimism at work can become so habitual and dominant that they perpetuate negativity in other places in our lives, and no one needs that bleed-over effect.

Then There's Personal Change

I think some of hardest changes to endure are those that impact us on a personal level, the kinds of changes that come unexpectedly with big consequences and perhaps even make us question our worthiness to receive our most basic needs to be loved and respected. Many have endured and come out the other side of changes like this. One encouraging lesson I have learned in traveling such bumpy roads is that we cannot always clearly understand the ultimate outcome of change. Haven't you also had an experience or two that has turned out for the better, even though at first blush it seemed to be an ominous threat? Things most often just seem to work out, even when they don't go according to our plan.

Change is an element that propels us into new realms of experience. It challenges our precious notions of how things ought to be, and calls us to rise to new abilities, new thoughts and new ideas. So here's my view: change can be an incredible catalyst for more—more growth, more valuable experiences and greater understanding, all of which can enhance our success. Change, when I decide to embrace it and follow its lead, can create a life that's even better than before.

It would seem logical then that we would be excited by the possibilities and embrace the idea of change, but this is often not the case. We prefer the predictability of things we know and understand. It's the fear of meeting a devil we don't know, doubting our ability to navigate less familiar territory. We may more often choose the easy route, sticking with the one bird in the hand rather than go after the two in the bush. As a result, we often end up feeling half full, because one bird was not really enough, all because we wanted to avoid the risk entailed when reaching for greater gains. If we can shift our attitude to one of being excited about adventuring and exploring new possibilities, we can find a surprising strength within us and more often than not rise to the occasion. Even if we don't, we will learn things of value in the process.

Enhancing personal excellence and building our life legacy will recurrently entail some degree of risk and bravery to navigate change in our lives. The willingness to release the one bird of predictability in order to make gains is part of the courage required to grow. Change is inevitable in our pursuits and our ability to acclimate to change determines success or failure. We need only look at successful people in history to appreciate their gift of adaptability. They embrace and creatively navigate the changing landscape they find themselves in and they trust their talents. They control what they can, are flexible in their thinking, and apply effort where they can influence outcomes. Having such a perspective provides us with the calmness and clarity to deploy our innate talents to make lemonade out of lemons.

And Then There's The Kind Of Change That Turns Our World Upside-down

Gargantuan changes can have us feeling as though we are coming undone. They can come in many forms; life-threatening illnesses, the death of a significant other, a divorce, loss of a job or having a financial crisis are to name a few. You may think bearing them and rising from those ashes entail more than the approaches I have written of, but the principles are the same. Somewhere inside you, you already possess the ability. It's just that such events seem so big we cannot see anything but the blackness of our despair, giving us the perception we are without power to experience anything other than pain, grief, shame, loneliness or whatever the manifestation of our suffering. They also can take more time and effort than other recoveries, so patience and perseverance are necessary articles for the journey.

It was at first difficult to include the story of my firing in the book because of how I experienced it—betrayal, blame, shame and humiliation all played a part. It was also difficult to do so because it involved an employer I was wholeheartedly devoted to and it is difficult to speak frankly about what I see as their failures because I hold them in such high regard. I knew, however, that I needed to tell it because that kind of experience is not unique to me and because it was one of the hardest things I've been through and learned from.

As I had mentioned before, this had been an incredible company to work for. The training – fabulous; the people – incredible; the work—both humbling and strengthening. With their coaching and mentorship, I was able to achieve and perform at a level that had exceeded my most ambitious dreams and shaped my personal growth deeply. I had some struggles over the course of my employment there with some interpersonal conflicts, but the compassionate coaching I received to modify my shortcomings and the willingness to learn enabled me to navigate the difficulties. This molded me in powerful ways for the better.

At my last Christmas party there, my Medical Director said to me, "I want you to know that I lost sleep over who to give the award to this year," (he was referring to an annual, coveted recognition given out each year to one medical crew member,) "you and Kenny are both so exceptional." Kenny got the award, but hearing he had trouble deciding was enough for me to feel tremendous gratitude and pride for all I had achieved there. I felt tremendously humbled for having had the opportunity to make the difference in so many lives and extremely proud of the job we consistently delivered as a flight crew. I fully appreciated how, under their guidance, I was able to experience a level of satisfaction and exhilaration I had not experienced before. The experience defined for me what excellence in practice was, and I came to understand what it takes to achieve it. I was supported in honing to a precise edge my own brand of being an excellent flight nurse. It also taught me that excellence is an inextricable part of living in the sweet-spot.

I still feel enormously appreciative of my employment experience there and it was the loss of that job which became the catalyst inspiring me to write this book. And despite the lack of a graceful departure strategy, the years I spent in that job will forever be one of my career's crown jewels and I still preserve friendships from that time. I deeply admired, respected and supported my company. I felt after many years of nursing employers, I had finally found a place where the patients always came first—a solid, immutable core value of my own that I shared in full partnership with them.

It's always hard to fully describe events that lead to the demise of a relationship. There are subtleties and nuances that are difficult to convey to illustrate in full measure what transpired. There is also a feeling of nakedness and vulnerability to honestly recount the part I played in my termination, but my purpose in telling it is to share how I survived it, how I endured the unjust pieces of it and how when leaning into the difficulty of accepting it, I learned, grew and became something more and better.

So let me set the stage. I had been based in a location that, like many flight personnel, I had to travel a long distance to get to. This was not a bad deal when considering it was only once a week I made that trip, worked a twenty-four hour shift, stayed with local friends for one night, then had another twenty-four hour shift, flying commercially home in the morning after getting off duty. I had been doing this for more than five years and it worked. I had a high degree of pediatric and neonatal transports in that location which pushed my learning edges, and had plenty of trauma and challenging critical care adult transports. I had honed my craft to a high degree, I was learning new things all the time given the company's drive to always strive for more. I was loving what I did more than I'd loved any career assignment. Simply put, it was exhilarating to practice at this level and I very much looked forward to going to work.

At the time, our smallish company of five bases began to expand. We began merging with other companies, opening bases across state lines and in locations more than 600 miles from our headquarters. The most difficult piece of rapid organizational growth, particularly when operations are far from corporate, is to perpetuate original core values and principles. These core ideas and values were what made it so successful, personally fulfilling and so different from other organizations I had either worked for or knew about.

My boss came to me one day saying, "Hey CJ, I have a proposition for you. The base we opened six months ago near where you live is having a few issues. You bleed what this company is all about and cultivate it. What would you think about going down there, helping us assess what the issues are and turning that around to be what our company is all about?" I was flattered. After all, this boss and I had been paired for many years and was a mentor to me when I had challenges. Further confirmation came from the next administrative level up, encouraging me to take on the challenge. Here was a chance to thank them and my company for all that I appreciated and also be a part of correcting a problem.

There were some reservations on my part however. The base was known to be having significant personnel difficulties. Some team members who had worked there referred to it as a "snake pit"...did I really want to go there? Being closer to home made it enticing and less expense to travel to. My other worry was my own personality. Would I be patient with those who didn't support the company or value its principles? My style of communication is very direct—sometimes overly so—which not everyone can appreciate. Had my communication skills evolved to a point where I could effectively communicate with those that needed to be turned around? I quelled these concerns because my superiors thought me capable, so I took the opportunity and bravely ventured forth.

Things were rough from the start and the unrest at that base was palpable. It was mostly unrecognizable as the company I loved. Some staff I would describe as vicious, conniving and overtly rude. It was a culture shock to see people treat others that way. They clearly had ideas about who I was without even bothering to get to know me. Some behaviors I witnessed were hard to believe, such as not being truthful in chart records and completely unprofessional behaviors when conflict arose. Their youth and immaturity were evident. Many of the company standards were lax and people resented me when I asked for compliance.

The company had hired a new supervisor for the base and though he had little exposure to our company and its values, we originally got along fine. I would inform my new boss of my observations as I had been asked to and he would make expectations clear, but that just fueled the staff's fire. I did my best to be patient, but some just dug in their heels further and were eventually terminated. Though we had weeded out the worst of the lot before the year was over, the terminations left the remnants feeling uneasy and self-protective.

The evolution of events that led up to my termination was somewhat subtle over the next two-year period. As time passed my new boss began to interpret company rules in his own rogue style and I made my objections known. There were times he did not follow company policies and in spite of trying to rectify it with him directly, there were times I felt compelled to ask other administrative people for assistance to get us on track, which of course he resented. He then took exception to other things, like disciplining me for being "out of uniform" when some firefighters came to the base for a training. It was 110 degrees in the hanger and I had unzipped my flight suit to my waist, removed the top half and tied the sleeves around my waist. I was of course wearing a black crew neck T shirt underneath, but he took exception to it. There also was a team of nurses on another shift who stirred up trouble unnecessarily. One of them, who had been identified as falsifying records, would not hesitate to give false accusations as well. Even though others who were present during those cited events came to my defense, it didn't seem to matter to my new boss.

I was pushing hard, too hard, to preserve the company values and felt that he was not exemplifying them with our community or with our employees. I fought the adage that a manager's bigger stick wins, I felt certain that if I stuck to what the preceding years had taught me about this company, I would prevail. What followed was a he-said-she-said conflict where he disparaged my motives and actions. To the upper echelon, if the boss says it, it must be true, right? I think they were too busy with expansion plans to pay much attention. Given our geographic distance from the company headquarters, I can understand it was difficult for them to verify what actually was happening.

He ultimately exercised his termination rights as a manager for the offense of my leaving work before a chart was completed. I had written my nursing notes and my partner was finishing the demographics so I thought it was reasonable to leave though I knew company policy said charts were to be finished before crew members leave. This early leaving was something I had *not once* exercised in my entire seven-plus years there and I would intentionally not schedule things the day after a shift because of our clock-out time being so unpredictable. On this occasion however, my mother had suffered a stroke earlier in the month and because I missed shifts at my hospital per diem job, I had gotten into a position of having to pick up a hospital shift that day to maintain my per diem obligations. I reasoned that no one in the history of the company had ever been fired for that sole offense, disciplined yes, but not terminated, so I took the risk. The two malicious females reported it to our boss and that was all he needed. He asked me about it, I told the truth, but none of my circumstances seemed to matter to him. No verbal or written warnings, just fired. Such is the world of "at will" employment.

I was stunned. I had always associated firing with abject failure. I had judged others for being fired, even when I didn't know the circumstances. I had a naïve belief that if I was good at my job and as a person, I could not possibly be let go from a job given my long-standing history of being diligent. I felt betrayed that my dearly-loved company allowed it. I had been defending it, wanting it preserved in all its integrity. Hadn't I consistently sought to uphold the standards as laid out by the company? I wasn't lying about circumstances, so how could this be? Most horrifying of all was the worry that people would judge me, as I had judged others!

I could only conclude the upper management didn't have a clear picture. A few days after I did call the Chief of Operations, a person I had a good relationship with, and unloaded all the details of what had transpired and what my boss had been up to. Some of the report I had previously withheld because I knew they were inflammatory enough to degrade my relationship with my boss even further. I had hoped to mend it to a reasonable degree by minimizing conflict, thinking I was picking my battles wisely.

I will of course never know what the COO thought of that conversation. What I do know is that my boss and the HR employee assisting him were terminated several weeks after me. I also know that a man of such low integrity can get himself in plenty of trouble without me and if they started watching carefully, all would be evident.

For many months after, all of these ideas of the injustice shown me circulated consciously and unconsciously, keeping me in a place of bitterness, insecurity, embarrassment and the kind of distrust that comes from what felt like betrayal and abandonment from those who should have had my back. I was preoccupied with feeling victimized and worrying about "When will the next rat unjustly take me down?" I finally realized I was giving away all my personal power by not taking steps to process this event in a valuable, positive way. My work was to undo the victim shackles, rise above it and evolve in a meaningful way that benefited my future.

As I began to evaluate the experience, I started to see that I had some very important lessons to learn. The event prompted a deep-dive into what part I had to play in it going so far south. I could see how my view of and relationship with authority figures, the use of my own power, communication with others, and my own lack of humility at times all played a part. More and more came into view, some even years later through the process of writing this book. I researched. I read multiple books, talked to people I thought wiser than me, studied actions of the successful, meditated, prayed for guidance and I became increasing skilled at mindfulness. The first baby step was understanding that it was limiting to view getting fired as a failure and as something done to me. Many companies don't like wave-makers, even when it is justified, and will often choose to rid themselves of the person raising alarm rather than fix the problem. I was the one who failed to recognize the choice point when it arrived to either adapt or move on. No company is perfect, and neither am I.

All of the factors surrounding this event tested and ultimately strengthened my own integrity and reinforced my own character. After emerging on the other side of that particular knothole, there was a clarity of vision far greater than I had before about how I wanted to be in the world and what I want to contribute to it.

The power and strength to return to a successful, happy life was created when I shifted my perception of things. Honestly owning my part, releasing the resentments and embracing the here and now were pivotal in enabling me to rise above it and move forward. It was only then I was able to shift my viewpoint. Instead of viewing being fired as a humiliating failure, I began viewing the event as feedback. As Edison once wisely observed, I could choose to learn from *what didn't work.* I also took comfort in something the Dali Lama said, "You only lose if you don't keep the lesson."

It took time to gain that insight, change perspective and fully own my piece of this. Believe me, I had many who supported me in harboring grudges and encouraged me to seek legal action for the injustice of it, but I felt it would just be a yucky place in which to be living and would hinder me in moving forward. Besides, the Universe has its own way of settling injustices and those involved will get their own lessons as It sees fit. It was in this way I was able to release the emotion around it and move forward.

I also learned that while it is important to be courageous, take on projects to effect change, and act in ways that support the improvement of our organizations, I have to choose carefully the where, when and how and accept the inherent risk of doing so. There are times, try though we may to make it work, we have to be wise enough to leave if we cannot make the necessary adjustments to be pulling together *with* the people around us. The reason is this: no one achieves the pinnacle of personal excellence or lives in the sweet-spot as an island. The context of where we are and the relationships we have there do matter. Creating synergy with those around us motivates us to a collective success.

I also underestimated the effect of quiet influence, being the change we wish to see, as Gandhi said. Someone pursuing excellence must be willing to exert whatever influence they have to continually move toward being better, inspiring those around them to do the same by example. At some point we may reach the limit of non-confrontational influence and have to decide if we wish to continue pushing where confrontation now exists. It can take time and consistent application of effort that we may, or may not, have the aptitude or willingness for. And there is risk, especially if the confrontations are with those who out-rank you. This is the point we have to consciously choose what it will be—push, adapt or bow out—and have our eyes wide open to the potential consequences of each choice. I have come to accept that I will always be a champion for best practices and that sometimes has a price that I am committed to paying.

I resisted all the indicators that it was time for a change. I loved the job, the flying, the intensity of the care we gave. I was at the top of my game, feeling like I had arrived at the summit of my career and the synergy of excellence I enjoyed with my medic partner was extraordinary. I was also fifty-four and feeling the physical work demands affecting my health and marriage. The dynamics with my boss were definitely a problem, but

I wondered how I could possibly be happy in another job when *this was* the top of my mountain? I kept pushing for a return to the great experience previously with my company, failing to account fully for what was actually happening—too afraid to try something new, too impatient for change and not willing to really look at any of the negative influences the job was having on my own life. My ego was fully wrapped up in the pride of being an accomplished flight nurse, somehow thinking I would matter less if I did not hold that title. Had I bowed out, realizing the job was no longer a good fit and that I had limited ability to change the dynamics there, I would have avoided a lot of heart-ache and my leaving would have had a very different feel. I had a long love affair with the flight world, had a lot to be proud of, wonderful memories and experiences to take forward, but my perspective was that everything else was a step down and some sort of decline in my career.

Boy was I wrong! The truth is, no one ever knows if they are on the tallest mountain of their life. I certainly found a whole new world of opportunity and potential for growth in leaving that pinnacle. Though I still miss the flight job and many of the fine people there, I realize that where I went to next was a much better fit for my stage of life and things have improved in a mul-titude of ways since I have moved forward. After my flight career my life gained more flexibility of schedule and I became very active within my department working on projects that cultivated our staff's skills and our degree of excellence as we provide care in our busy emergency department. I had daily, meaningful con-nections with coworkers and patients, and starting to write this book had me satisfied and content. I'm was also home for din-ner every night and my relationship with my husband deepened because of it. I've learned so much from that event and it pro-pelled me into a new chapter in my career that deepened my love of and satisfaction with my work. My sweet-spot just got shinier though it looked completely different.

When we are brave and embrace change our vision expands. Resistance to it keeps us limited. Who we are in any snapshot in time is never a thing of finality, there will always be possibility for different and amazing experiences that delight and fulfill us. With this kind of openness and intention, we see and create possibility, thus making room to pursue other dreams and rise to other—perhaps even greater—potentials. No one can ever take away our talents and abilities; we just simply refuse to apply them when we choose to wallow in our failures. A Chinese proverb says, "Failure is not in the falling down, it is in the refusal to get up."

The Universe, God if you are a believer, will use whatever it takes to get our attention and help us grow. Spirit loves each and every one of us that much. Lessons recur until we learn the lesson. Health, work, relationships and money are just a few ways the curricula is communicated. The lessons come how they may—sometimes in unexpected or unimagined ways—but always opening new worlds of possibility.

It may take a leap of faith to trust this, but change is your friend, often having an uncanny timing of arrival just when a little shake-up of the norm can be the beginning of something exhilarating, new, and extraordinary. If we can create some excitement and a sense of adventure about the possibilities ahead, we are primed to succeed because we are open, optimistic and our creativity is unbound.

LIVING IN THE SWEET-SPOT

··· 22 ···

A Warrior With A Servant's Heart

"I think that we are too concerned with what we can get out of life, rather than what we give. I think it's God's plan for us to leave the world a better place."

Edythe Kirchmaier, 105-year-old woman being interviewed by Oprah

ONE OF MY favorite concepts I've coined from my experiences is *A Warrior with A Servant's Heart.* This has probably been the most powerful component for excelling and creating true satisfaction in my career. And before you parallel this concept with some sort of warring or aggressive stance, hear me out. Being a warrior in the sense I intend is the integration of being brave and prepared, coupled with the desire to be of service. Making the two concepts harmonize in my work life was the final key to creating a career I really loved. Even when up against difficulties in the ensuing years, my love of the job thrived. Then, I got smart enough to try it at home with my husband and family—whoa! A happy and rich life grew even more lush.

My Warrior Bootcamp

I believe we all have a warrior within. The faces differ in how that may show up, and some have it honed to a higher degree of effectiveness than others. Some of us feel born with it, others of us are catalyzed by life experiences. Some of us don't believe we have the warrior spirit. If you do not think of yourself as a warrior, let's dive into what I mean.

I think I have always been a warrior. Growing up with two brothers may have been part of it, competing with them since girls were scarce in my neighborhood. It was further honed when my family began to disintegrate when I was twelve, followed by having to redefine how life was to be when I left home at fourteen. The loss of that family grounding gave me an early realization that sometimes life was unjust, and that I had to fight for how I wanted my life to be. Viewing myself as a warrior gave me the courage to act. In the earlier stages of my life being a warrior rested more heavily on aggressive pursuit of my ideals and resulted in conflict because at the time, I simply did not know how to use my courage and strength properly. I viewed my battles in the classical warrior sense—to defeat the enemy. While I was always fighting for what I thought was right and just, the approach cost me dearly at times.

As I have matured, being a *wise* warrior means so much more. The battles are no longer about defeating something or someone; the battle is to continually advance myself closer to excellence and the goals I set for my life, along with what I feel is best for humanity as a collective.

Growing into a wise warrior led me to understanding that there are things we do around fear and self-preservation instincts generated from overblown or unnecessary feelings of vulnerability. It's *what I do with* circumstances, not what circumstances *do to me*. I am stronger and less vulnerable than I previously imagined. When I now apply my warrior-self, I am more clear-headed and can turn most any circumstance to my advantage if I use the courage to act rightly. It also means that when opportunity arises, I encourage those around me in those directions as well.

To me, being at work has often felt like a battleground. It is complicated, unpredictable, and requires I have my wits to keep myself and others safe. There is a fight in progress on many levels: against disease, for a patient's psychological well-being, maintaining my own well-being, demands for efficiency, to anticipate the disease's next move, etc. It's a battle requiring strategy, foresight and confident execution.

As a warrior nurse I think my responsibilities could be expressed like this:

- First: maintain my own fitness—mentally and physically—to carry out my duties.
- Second: commit to supporting noble causes.
- Third: be ever-ready to learn and expand who I am.
- Fourth: maintain my resourcefulness and remain flexible in how I accomplish goals.
- Fifth: continue to practice and hone my abilities and skills to an art.
- Sixth: have my coworker's six (have their back).
- Seventh: consistently do the right thing, even when it entails personal risk or is inconvenient.
- And lastly: have the self-discipline to manage my emotions when I find them getting in the way of my primary life objectives—to offer the highest quality care, live the life I imagine and make my relationships work.

I don't always get it right, but these are the wise warrior principles I strive for and revisit when I am off track.

Being a warrior requires bravery, a willingness to take risks to accomplish the desired outcome, and a willingness to push ourselves further even though we feel we have reached our limitations. There have been many warrior nurses in the history of nursing that been agents of change, shown we are capable, and have powerfully advanced the care we offer patients. These warriors will tell you setbacks of any sort can be a teacher, and the learning gained should immediately be deployed for further advancement as we battle for excellence. Any warrior will tell you there is exhilaration and pride in rising from the ashes and pushing forward for the greater good. In doing so we discover new things about ourselves, become braver in the process and are deeply gratified—at a soul level—by the effort.

A Servant's Heart

The best of warriors also cultivate a servant's heart. Being an exceptional warrior actually comes from the deep desire to serve. Everyone can experience burnout on occasion. It has been this concept of service to others that has taken me straight out of burnout and into a realm where I naturally became motived to pursue my best because it is important to serve others well. The focus became outward instead of inward on my own insecurities and the other "stuff" that clutters my mind and burdens my heart. It became more natural to ask, "How can I be of help?" Focusing on service also obliterates any self-wallowing I may be engaging in due to circumstances.

Being of service is a quality that is easily recognized in stories of heroism, but it can also manifest in the world of large corporations and their cultures. Most of us have flown on Southwest Airlines or have at least seen their logo, which is a heart with wings. While they are not perfect as the system failure in 2023 demonstrated, their story of company culture is well worth reading about. Their culture is built on a philosophy that if a person has a servant's heart, one that is consistently focused on how they can help others, great customer service will happen. I learned about this some years ago when I read the book, *The Southwest Way* where a couple of psychologists set out to study their cultural success.

Southwest trains their employees to offer service from a place of genuine caring and a commitment to excellence. Though they are a no frills kind of business, when I had a five-year stint of flying with them twice a week between 2005 to 2010, I can only recall three incidents where I thought the customer service was lacking. I had experience after experience of Southwest employees delivering not only a consistent product of traveling without a hitch, but they seemed, in large part, to enjoy their own part in creating it. Given this illustrious history, I can only imagine the great pain 2023 caused them. I have to wonder if the neglect shown to their system upgrade was directly related to the financial devastation of Covid to the travel industry, because from what I knew of them, it was totally out of character.

The key to this consistent delivery, the psychologists discovered, was to instill in employees a true desire to help others. In every way possible employees are encouraged to help passengers have an easy travel experience. To accomplish this, the organization focused on employees as their greatest asset. Every employee is directed to take time each day to focus on improvement and service. (This is where I learned of the reflective practice I have spoken about and its effectiveness has generated the habit to do so throughout the various parts of my life and in my relationships.) Through this active seeking to improve the company and themselves, they were better able to serve their customers and coworkers. It became readily apparent the employees' growing effectiveness became the company's "engine of motivation" – all because of the organization's core belief that employee achievements through great service are the company's most prized assets.

Gratitude is also high on the Southwest list and some of the ways in which they express this is to thank veterans over the PA when they are on the plane and through many corporate sponsored charitable works. They also consistently have a section in their magazine to showcase a frontline employee with a picture and short bio illustrating how their personal brand of excellence was in service to someone or something. What got them recognition is that they used their influence and time to go above and beyond to achieve something good which, I believe, is its own form of heroism.

Integrating the concept of a servant's heart into nursing is something I adopted after I read the Southwest Airlines book, which happened about twenty years into my career. What happened was unexpected. My satisfaction with all that I did, though sometimes gruelingly difficult, became enjoyable in ways I had not experienced before. It was a simple shift in perception, but the influence it had on me was profound. To this day, when I approach my work I strive to be in a place that's committed to having a servant's heart. Doing so consistently proves to be transformative in not only my relationships with others and my patients, it has exponentially added to my level of satisfaction. Caring for others and doing so with a servant's heart simply nurtures our truest nature, the DNA in us that is coded for community.

We certainly can do this in medicine and have the good fortune of the built-in motivator that what we do *really matters* in the grand scheme of things. Health is precious, fostering health is a privilege, and we are frequently recognized as one of the noblest professions. We see people in their most vulnerable states and take care of them when they must surrender a large degree of control. Reminding ourselves of this delicate position is a good way to keep in touch with a heart-oriented level of care.

We will never always get everything right, but when we consistently offer our best, we get a sense of achievement that allows us to forgive ourselves when we miss the mark. It's one of the best perks of consistently giving our best. It is a well-studied fact that care offered in this way will be perceived by our patients as excellent, even if there are hiccups along the way.

Pairing a warrior spirit with a servant's heart gives us the high-octane life experience we crave to feel complete. Make up your mind to be courageous and make a difference. Engage your heart to feel compassion for others and the breadth of your experience will continue to expand and your heart will be full. Make it a habit to be vigilant for opportunities to serve others in small ways. Focus outwardly on how you are a light in the world and can assist others. This unleashes the magic of the sweet-spot to happen in your own life.

The battles of life, which we all have, tell part of the story of creating the people we are today. Cherish these experiences, release any shame you may be holding on to when having to learn the hard way and use them to your advantage, trusting they had a purpose to make you stronger. Be deliberate as you assist others in a way where they too can be courageous and giving, remembering always that a true warrior consistently strives to serve and make the greatest difference possible with whatever tools are at hand.

··· 23 ···

We Will Never Be Done

"Life isn't about finding yourself, it's about creating yourself."

George B. Shaw

NO MATTER HOW much we grow, learn and evolve, we will never be done expanding our talents and abilities. Writing this book has taught me that. Like so many of the greats who are consistently driven to hone, improve and discover more, we also can view every day as a new adventure unfolding. Through every large and small experience of success or challenge, we can add to our treasure trove of talent.

Once I committed to and embraced my "learning edges" and this "never being done" business, the joy in life and career began to expand. I found myself more comfortable with life because I was living a place of acceptance and excited about what I may learn next or become better at doing. Life seems fuller, richer, more satisfying and—perhaps most importantly—I gained a greater ability to be fully present in the moment where I can take complete advantage of all the opportunities my moments held. It became exciting to always be learning and the fear of not being enough or knowing enough dissipated. It is in integrating this idea that we all can accept ourselves as evolving beings, where we become freer to accept our current circumstances and freer to foster our own evolution. In this mindset we can *relax into* the adventure of life.

It is also calming to know that life is not a race to some imagined finish line. It is instead a rousing exploration and creation of who we aspire to be, a vision of creation that is ever-evolving as we evolve. Wherever we are in life and career, it can have an immense effect when we fully accept our imperfect humanness and the nature of it being a journey. In that acceptance we can finally comprehend it simply does not serve us to "feel down" or "less-than" because of our circumstances, our imperfections and inability to *always* get it right. It is in embracing all of it, as we are, that we begin to calm our sense of struggle and begin our mastery of self. As we become this kind of courageous explorer, our focus expands and we begin to see the unlimited possibilities in the expected *and* the unexpected. In that mental shift we leave behind old ways of living and the habit of focusing on what life is lacking. It's exciting and freeing to wonder from this perspective, "What does this moment hold for me?" or, "What will I experience and learn today?"

Life has a natural tendency to take shape in amazing ways and contribute to our intentions when we live deliberately. We attract what we need when we don't cling tightly to exactly how we think things should be. Our job is to stay intentional, clear about our goals and acting in alignment with what we value—to "keep pitching" our best, as it were. In my own story, I can certainly attest that much has happened in the ten years it's taken me to write this book. Big internal shifts as well as the many changes going on in our world. My horizons continue to expand as I climb new mountain tops. My views have shifted and my happiness continues to deepen. It may surprise you to know that I left western medicine in 2021 and now work in a naturopathic clinic doing infusions, holistic therapies, Reiki and coaching patients in healthy practices. I absolutely love the work and the doctor I work for. She's brilliant, funny and a good teacher for this new world I'm in. The environment is collaborative and my experience in critical care is utilized as we assist patients in sorting through their issues. We are a happy group and it's not uncommon to hear laughter. We spend time with our patients and the environment of care we provide has patients feeling well cared for. What I am doing and how we are doing it feels well aligned with my personal values and beliefs so passion for the work comes easily.

Leaving my critical care career was a rocky departure, lots of self-doubt and uncertainty, but what emerges on the other side of every experience is largely up to us. How we manage our thoughts toward that which is constructive, and what we do with the occurrences that present themselves, are the largest predictors of outcome. If we take a misstep or become maladaptive in our thoughts and acts, through conscious living we are reminded to saddle-up, work to reframe to the positive, and try again. It is about putting *all our experiences to use* for our own clarity about life, working to modify not-so-good traits and habits and using events to motivate us to higher ground—*that* is the daily work. Even accepting the folks we are not fond of or have wronged us, or bravely reflecting on life experiences to better understand our part in what went wrong—it is in these types of processes that we allow the blacksmith of life-experience to forge who we are today and who we become tomorrow. I am grateful for those experiences, even though at times the hammering was painful.

Surrounding ourselves with aspiring and inspiring people is a powerful practice as well, for the company we keep shapes our habits and thoughts. I've heard it said that we are the average of the five people we choose to spend the most time with. Are we choosing friends and associates wisely? Our enjoyment and mastery of life is enhanced when we have the kind of friends who are also striving for growth and are wise enough to know that loving us includes fostering our own accountability in life when we fall short of walking our talk. Nothing can compare to a trusted friend who will remind us of what we value most and "hold our feet to the fire" when life challenges us and the giving of our best or doing the right thing becomes difficult.

One such friend is Gail, who I had the good fortune to meet at my first writing seminar. Serendipitously, she is also a nurse, though in a much different way than I, working as a psychiatric facilities administrator. Our connection was instant and our quest to complete our respective books continued through a series of writing retreats at a cottage in Pacific Grove, California.

We would sit for hours immersed in our own writing, but at times we would engage in thoughtful discussions that had a synergistic effect on our endeavors, often revealing profound truths and understanding, or further clarifying what we already suspected was true. Sometimes the conversations would be about concepts or portions of our books, other times about issues that we were wrestling with in our lives. They often included eruptions of laughter, at other times we would sit in stunned silence, digesting the insight we had just arrived at, mesmerized by the clarity of "getting it" through our process of honest dialogue. She knows the truth of her own continual development and living a life aligned with her values, and we will forever remain the kind of friends who are courageous enough to speak honestly to each other and assist one another to stay on track.

We often discussed how having *the willingness to positively embrace life*—with all its uncertainties, fears, unexpected events, imperfections and discoveries—and *our commitment to offer our best, nurture ourselves, give time to breathe, flex and grow no matter what comes our way,* fuels us toward more and better. These are the basic bottom-line precepts that provide us with the rich sense of a life and career well lived. Life will still come unhinged at times, but our resilience and resourcefulness will be greatly enhanced by these strategies and can bestow on us a deeper contentment in life.

We are indeed astute if we let go of a very human desperateness to finally arrive and be done for it really is as elusive as the proverbial cool mirage to a thirsty desert traveler. The truth is, if we ever think we have attained all we can in life and are done growing, it is in that moment that we will truly begin dying. When we believe there is no more to discover and things are as good as they'll get, it creates a blindness where we fail to let anything more in, believing there is no more to see, learn or do. Such a position makes us incapable of noticing the delightful, unexpected gifts along the ordinary roads we're traveling and incapable of progress toward even greater happiness. When we think we are done, it diminishes our ability to experience gratitude, joy and all the feelings that come with new discoveries, experiences and achievements. Living with an inherent excitement for growth is the alchemy that converts our ordinary lives into extraordinary adventures.

Let me leave you with one last consideration. We may have concluded that the only real sense of completion in our lives occurs after we have breathed our final breath and can no longer catalog any new mortal experiences. I would have you consider this: *even then* who we had been on this earth will still be undertaking more. Where we have been, what we have done and how we have coexisted in the world leaves behind our fingerprints, forever left on the lives we have touched, living on in ways unexpected, continuing to influence the world we had lived in. Each fingerprint has the potential of a seed and each can produce a legacy, so let's be determined to give our best and make them good ones. You matter, and especially as a caregiver to the human race, you have daily, potent impact in this world.

The only question remaining is, what else will you do with this extraordinary, wildly precious life of yours? Go ahead. Apply your own wise and wonderful brand of excellence, watch the magic of it unfold and savor living in The Sweet-Spot.

● ● ●

More ways for expansion found on my website: *cjsnow.net*

Integrity Exercise: Clarifying And Aligning With Your Core Values

Get paper and pen. Read each step through before taking action.

Step One: Take a few minutes to write down as many core values you think of, (at least twenty) that are important and believe a truly admirable person would possess. Include those you know are already strong in your own life and those you would like to be more evident. Consider both your personal and your work life. Avoid self-evaluation at this point about where you are with each, just brainstorm, do it quickly with free-flowing thought. Write down all those that you believe are important, big and small alike. They may be things like honesty, compassion, efficiency, balance, bravery, light-heartedness, kindness, showing love, taking ownership, connection with God/Higher Power/ Spirit, personal fitness, spending time in nature, competence, self-awareness, commitment, keeping your word, having faith, truthfulness, loyalty, fairness or justice—I could go on, but you get the idea. Twenty may seem like a lot, but the point is to dig a little so you find the bits and piece that you believe are important. Complete this list before reading further.

Step Two: This part takes honesty and considerable reflection. Carefully look at each value you've listed and think about how you may or may not be emulating it well in your own life. Which ones would you like to strengthen in your life? Which ones have you drifted from a bit? Underline the ones you want to tune-up and/or strengthen.

Step Three: Pick the top five from those you have underlined that you believe are *the <u>most</u> important for you to have more of* in the context of your life and/or your work. Circle these. They may even be the ones you try to talk yourself out of because it is uncomfortable to acknowledge them as important or they seem too difficult to accomplish. Neatly write those circled values on a separate sheet of paper, set them aside for later and go to the next step.

Step Four: Now you are going to rate your current satisfaction with your life as it is now. **This IS NOT about whether you've achieved your goals or the dream job. It IS NOT about having enough money or whether you have your true love.** Instead, it is about your *overall contentment or sense of well-being*. This takes a little introspection and careful consideration. When evaluating this, think about your moods throughout the past month, how often have you felt uplifted, at ease, peaceful; and, how often you may have felt anxious, ambivalent or simply "checked out" in diversions like TV, shopping, playing games on your phone or other entertainment. It's not that those activities are symptomatic of an unhappy life, I'm just asking that you notice when you do them out of boredom or wanting to escape discontentment. Dissatisfaction could also manifest as wishing you were somewhere else, feeling regret, anxiety or drinking too much. You can be completely honest because this is a private exercise.

Now, using a scale of one to ten, ten being 100% fulfilled with all that you hold dear, feeling happy and at peace no matter where you are or what you are doing, satisfied with how your life is and feeling totally confident that your life experience could not be improved upon. Remember, we **are not** talking about the amount of money or things you have here. Pick the number that is an overall representation of your level of satisfaction with *who you are as a person* and *your sense of well-being as you are living your current life*. Take your time, be thoughtful as you give yourself a rating.

Step Five: As you look at your self-evaluation number, you may notice that your level of happiness directly correlates with how well you are emulating the core values you circled as most important to improve upon. If you rated yourself as a nine or greater, congratulations...you are among the minority in today's world.

If you rated yourself less than a nine, you have plenty of company. Thankfully, to improve your score is fairly simple. Take the sheet of paper with the five values you've written down and focus over the next three to six weeks by applying yourself to this little tune-up project. Read them over at least once a day, or more often if you think it helpful. Create an action plan in your mind or on paper about how these values can be incorporated and expanded in your day-to-day living. Think about what specific thoughts, words or deeds you can do to make your life principles more alive and in harmony with what you want more of. If you want to improve your kindness, commit to five random acts of kindness a day for example, and review your progress before you go to bed; or, you could create some affirmations to use through the day which target those values. Using Post-It notes or phone reminders is helpful. A practice I routinely use when I feel there is something to improve is to set aside five minutes each morning to visualize how the desired values can be displayed in my life through thought, word or deed. If I forget to take the action or somehow miss the mark, I simply, without judgement, reset my course and try again. That kind of intentionality can fast-track us at surprising speed where we soon realize the desired endpoint has actually become a habit.

Step Six: The more you tune things up, the higher you are likely to rate your level of satisfaction. So here we test the theory. Be deliberate in your improvement in small or big ways, and assign a new score in three to six weeks to your overall satisfaction and sense of well-being. Share your observations on my website, cjsnow.net.

For continued support in your journey,
please visit my website for many resources
to inspire your own brand of excellence.
cjsnow.net

About The Author

Carolyn Julia "CJ" Snow was inspired toward medicine first by her beloved grandfather, a small-town physician. She graduated first as a paramedic in 1980 and then obtained her Bachelor's in Nursing in 1988. CJ's love of Critical Care Medicine kept her working in Emergency Departments, Intensive Care Units, and in Critical Care Transport as a Flight Nurse, maintaining dual national board certifications in Emergency and Intensive Care Nursing (C.E.N. and C.C.R.N.) for over three decades. With her experience in various leadership roles, at the bedside in world-class hospitals, and as an educator in her specialties, she brings a perspective that straddles many points of view. Triumphs and hardships have all been her teachers, but it is her tireless desire to hone her clinical expertise and personal life skills that make her a natural innovator, leader, and visionary with an authentic, motivating voice.

1980

2024

2010

www.ingramcontent.com/pod-product-compliance
Lightning Source LLC
Chambersburg PA
CBHW052036090426
42739CB00010B/1934